I BOUGHT MY HOUSE
WITH CREDIT CARDS

By

G. Earl Rustia Miranda

I Bought My House with Credit Cards

INTRODUCTION

Why is this how-to book different? Unlike other books in the business and finance realm, I will tell you my secrets in the first chapter. There is no need to read through hundreds of pages to get to the secret knowledge you desire. Of course, you might just think I am insane once I reveal my simple secret.

Through my own experiences with the credit card companies, I knew it would not be long before my wife would start being harassed by phone. I knew she did not have the funds for the minimum payments on all of her credit cards. She needed a lower-interest rate so she would eventually pay off all of her credit cards. I thought that a home equity line of credit that was just what she needed. Unfortunately, she needed a large home equity line of credit. The home equity line of credit had to be big enough to swallow up all of her high-interest credit card debt. Finding the home equity line would be the key to the solution. With that in mind, my wife and I started looking for a bigger house.

That was when I bought my new house using credit cards. Of course, I did not present my Visa™ or MasterCard™ to the real estate agent. No doubt, the real estate agent would have just laughed at me.

How did I do it? Most major credit cards give you the option to get a "cash advance". Essentially, you are given credit card checks that can be deposited into any checking or savings account. These credit card checks can be written for any amount and are added to your credit card balance for the next billing cycle.

Most of you already know this. If that is indeed the case, why aren't you depositing these credit card checks into your bank accounts so you can buy real estate? I realize that this sounds crazy, but it really did work.

Is it risky? Of course, it is. I won't lie to you. Will the credit reporting agencies see that you are adding more debt? Of course, they will. Fortunately for you, credit reporting agencies can take up to thirty days to process this information. In the meantime, you can deposit these checks into your bank account. If you are lucky, you can cover the costs of the down payment, escrow, and closing costs on your new real estate acquisition. Yes, you are essentially borrowing the principal, the down-payment, and all the other costs associated with buying real estate. This is my version of 100% financing.

Gee, that sounds so simple and straightforward. Be forewarned, though. There are a lot of pitfalls and time is not on your side. As with everything in life, the execution of the plan is just as important as the plan itself. There will be many temptations to use these credit card checks for other reasons, so you must be disciplined.

What is stopping you from buying a home? Sure, your circumstances may be different. Not everyone is prior or current military. You might even have a healthy bank account. If you are currently renting an apartment, do you know that you are helping the owner pay for the mortgage *(loan from the bank)* on his apartment building? After thirty years, the apartment building will be his free and clear. What will you have after thirty years of paying rent? How will you pay for rent after you finally retire?

In this book, you will discover that there is really is a way to buy a house with "no money down". Other books will ask you to find sellers who are desperate to sell. From these sellers, these books want you to negotiate a "no money down" sale. These sellers will ultimately provide 100% owner financing just to unload their property. In my experience, finding a seller who wants to sell that desperately is like winning the lottery. The deal may be wonderful for you, but do you really want to buy their property? Sellers only do 100% owner financing when they have exhausted every other method of attracting buyers.

With this book, I will show you a better way to use credit cards. I will show you how to borrow the down payment and closing costs from your credit cards. You will not be searching for the right seller for a fantastic deal. Instead, you can get a fair deal from any seller. Technically, it would not be 100% owner financing. Instead, it will be 80% bank financing and 20% borrowed from your own credit cards. It will take timing and discipline, but it is entirely possible to buy a house using your own credit cards. All you need is the knowledge in this book.

Before I go any further, I want make something very clear. With the exception of material quoted from other sources, the content of this book is based exclusively on the author's personal experience. Before trying any of the ideas in this book, I urge you to check with your lawyer and/or tax professional. Laws dealing with debt, revolving credit, taxes, insurance, and banking vary from state to state. Laws change all the time. The author does not provide any legal or tax advice. The author is not a lawyer or tax professional. Always verify first. Check the fine print, because the credit card companies, banks, and lending institutions have the law and the politicians on their side. You and I do not have that advantage, but you do have this book. Read on.

I Bought My House with Credit Cards

HIGH DRAMA

Back before the Great Recession of 2007-2009, I was sitting with a loan officer at one of the major banks. My wife had $40,000 in credit card debt. Before I came to the bank, I had calculated the minimum payment on her credit cards. I discovered that by paying only the minimum payment on her credit cards would never allow her to pay off her obligations. I was very worried. To make matters worse, the minimum payments on all her credit cards amounted to a whopping $355 each month. That amount was more than my car payment.

I was desperate. I needed a way to consolidate all of her credit debt. I also needed to get a better interest rate if I had any chance of paying off her credit card debt. Thus, I told the bank officer that I needed a home equity line of credit to pay off her credit cards.

"Sorry, sir," said the loan officer, "We can only give you a home equity line of credit for $20,000."

"Is there any way to increase that home equity line of credit?" I asked.

"No," said the loan officer, "You've only been in your house for a few years."

"What do I need to do to get more?" I asked.

"Do you have any other collateral?" asked the loan officer.

I tried not to panic. My mind raced. I had to think quickly.

"I have a handful of silver half-dollars and an old car," I said.

"We can probably get you a personal line of credit," said the loan officer, "But that would only be for a few thousand dollars or more."

The loan officer looked down at the paperwork. He saw that I had an old Mercury that was almost paid off. He was not interested in the silver coins.

"I'm sorry," said the loan officer, "But that's all we can do for you."

I felt no malice from the loan officer. In fact, he sympathized with my plight. Quietly, he waited for me to speak, because there was nothing else he could do for me.

"What do you suggest I do?" I asked.

The loan officer looked through the paperwork carefully before answering my question. He suggested that my wife and I go get credit counseling. From his experience, we were not the only ones facing such dire financial problems due to credit card debt. He stressed that there was nothing more he could do.

"To borrow more money against your house," said the loan officer, "You need a bigger house."

I was stunned by the loan officer's answer. It took me a while to finally accept the loan officer's advice. He was right. Banks and lending institutions need collateral. My borrowing power depended solely on my collateral.

I Bought My House with Credit Cards

In the end, I bought a bigger house. Luckily, I was able to borrow more against the larger house to pay off my wife's credit cards. With the larger home equity line, I rolled all of the credit card debt into the home equity line. As a result, I had only one payment at a lower interest rate. With the lower interest rate, I was able to pay off the debt in less time. Eventually, the harassing phone calls from the credit card companies stopped. There was no need to declare bankruptcy. Even better than that, we were able to sleep better. We were on the road to less debt.

I Bought My House with Credit Cards

WHAT IS REAL ESTATE?

What is real estate? In short, real estate is land. In most places in the world, real estate is a specific area measurement of the earth plus everything above and below. In theory, a piece of real estate extends to the skies above and to the earth's core below.

In states like Texas and Oklahoma, the earth below the surface is not immediately sold with the surface of the earth. In these states, the major industries revolve around oil and gas. Since oil and gas is extracted from deep in the ground, the earth below is very valuable. The remains of the dinosaurs have been crushed for thousands of years. Their remains have become black, bubbling goo. From this antediluvian goo, modern refineries extract natural gas, gasoline, and plastic.

In fact, real estate transactions in Texas and Oklahoma do not normally include the earth below the surface. Usually, the earth below the surface is sold as mineral rights. Sure, the earth below is the realm of worms and burrowing creatures, but the hunt for fossil fuels will always make this real estate valuable. It is literally buried treasure for the lucky few.

In New York, another form of real estate is highly prized, too. It is the real estate above the earth where we walk. According to Bruce Harwood's <u>Real Estate Principles</u>, an air right is "the right to occupy and use the airspace above the surface of a parcel of land". With air rights, developers can build above existing buildings. Telecommunication companies can use the rooftops of tall buildings to construct giant microwave towers to send out cellular phone signals. In the same way, large-scale television antennae can also be placed on the tops of multi-story buildings. These antennae deliver digital and analog signals to our television sets.

What does this all mean for us? Real estate is valuable. It is also unique. When one buys real estate, one buys a specific parcel of land. There is no other piece of land like it because of its location. Unlike other valuable items you can own, the location of real estate never changes.

Back in ancient Egypt, farmers had a hard time determining the location of their plot of land. Every year, the banks of the Nile would overflow. Rich earth was deposited everywhere. The silt from the Nile made crops grow, but it made finding one's plot of land almost impossible. The silt covered everything. Over time, the Egyptians developed advanced mathematics to re-trace the location of each person's plot of land. The Egyptians would start at a certain place. From there, the Egyptians would measure the exact direction and distance to each point of each corner of each farmer's plot of land. Thus, the fertile silt was welcomed each year. Each year, the Nile overflowed its banks. With advanced mathematics, each farmer was able to retrace and rediscover their own individual plot of land. Without delay, they could once again plant their crops in the same place.

Today, the study of locating and verifying plots of land is called surveying. The ancient Egyptian methods are still used today. However, surveying has been enhanced with computers and lasers for unparalleled accuracy.

I Bought My House with Credit Cards

What does this mean for us? Real estate is one-of-a-kind, because the location is unlike any other. In certain locations, real estate is an ever-decreasing commodity. In New York City, there is only so much space to build. The competition to acquire land is fierce. If you wanted to build a house in New York City, you would have to compete with millions of other people. In fact, no one builds single-family homes in the city of New York anymore. Since the price of real estate is so high in New York City, people build multi-story, multi-family buildings. These multi-family buildings offset the high price of land. In comparison, the State of Alaska allowed people to build in the wilderness free of charge. The government had done this to entice people to settle in the State of Alaska. There was a lack of people wanting to brave the frozen tundra. The State of Alaska needed people to challenge the abundance of natural predators. Thus, the government waived the price of the land.

For the purposes of this book, I am asking you to consider real estate somewhere between these two extremes. If you do live in a location where the government has incentives to settle the land and to build a house, this book is not for you. By all means, take charge and find yourself a plot of land. Live free of charge and enjoy a mortgage-free homestead.

For most of us, housing is a different situation. Renting an apartment can drain a budget each month. Indeed, rent money can sometimes take up to half of our paycheck. In a large metropolitan area, this is normal.

What do you get after thirty years of rent payments? When you finally retire, where will you live? Will you have enough money to pay the rent after you retire? Even though it is a daunting task, owning a house should be part of everyone's long-term plan for financial well-being. For most people, retirement usually means not working. Even if you don't want to stop working, employers may force you to retire. You may develop health problems due to age. You might even lose your job because your employer wants a younger, tech-savvy staff.

Do you really want to find a less expensive apartment in a seedier part of town because you are no longer employed? Let's face it. Most of us don't save enough for retirement anyway. That tiny annuity from your employer might not be able to make the monthly rent payment. Even if you have a stellar retirement plan, there is no guarantee that retirement money can keep up with your present lifestyle.

If you're smart about it, you can probably find a small house. This small house can have a mortgage payment close to your present rent payment. If you live in a major metropolitan area, there are always apartments or condominiums being sold every day. Sure, there are additional rules when you buy apartments from a co-op. Sure, there would be homeowner's association dues tacked onto the monthly mortgage payment. Still, many of their rules may already apply to where you are currently renting. Of course, you may need to live further away from work, but most metropolitan areas have public transportation. The bus or train may take longer to get to your work. Still, it is a small inconvenience compared to the peace of mind knowing you will have a place to retire someday.

I Bought My House with Credit Cards

GOVERNMENT MONEY

What if I don't want to borrow the down payment? That's fine. If you've been in the military, you may not need to borrow the down-payment and the closing costs. In fact, there are new "no down-payment" programs created specifically for returning soldiers, sailors, and airmen. Be sure to tell your bank or lending institution that you are a veteran. There are always government programs for returning veterans. When most banks and lending institutions cannot lend you money, the government may have a program to help you acquire your own home. For those of you who are still renting, these are no down-payment mortgages aimed specifically at veterans.

After World War Two, government programs were created to allow returning veterans a chance to get a home loan. Millions of veterans were coming back, but there was nowhere for them to live. The government wanted desperately to return these servicemen to the workforce. The United States had a mountain of war debt and they needed additional revenue. If the returning servicemen did not have adequate housing, the returning servicemen would not be paying taxes.

During the Great Recession of 2007-2009, many veterans found themselves with homes they could not sell. Unlike civilians, military personnel do not have much control over their job assignments. They don't have a choice if they are given assignments in a different city. As a result, they are often burdened with two mortgages. Their previous home would remain unsold for years at a time. With two mortgages, many military families found themselves in trouble. This created a tremendous strain on their marriages. With war in the Middle East and suicides on the rise, the government once more decided to provide veterans with no down-payment loans. These loans were never widely advertised, because the general public placed the blame for the Great Recession of 2007-2009 on these no down-payment loans.

At the same time, Navy Federal Credit Union initiated a "no down-payment" program, too. This credit union caters to current and previous military personnel. In fact, their board of directors is usually comprised of current and retired military officers. No doubt, their board of directors heard the pleas from their credit union members for no-hassle, no down-payment loans.

In contrast to other banks and lending institutions, Navy Federal Credit Union can count on the continuous stream of income from the government. Each month, thousands of servicemen receive direct deposits from the government. Unlike civilians, current military personnel do not worry so much about their next paycheck. This allowed Navy Federal Credit Union to initiate no down-payment loans with greater confidence. With offices at every Navy training base, Navy Federal Credit Union enjoys a lack of competition from civilian banks. If you are lucky enough to belong to this venerable institution, I recommend inquiring about their new loan programs.

Even before this, the Veteran's Affairs administration had a no down-payment program, too. Like the Navy Federal Credit Union, these home-buying incentives were originally designed for returning veterans. As with all VA loan programs, the government provides a guarantee to the primary lender. If the borrower defaults, the government would step in to pay off the loan. Of course, there is a funding fee associated with this type of loan. True, there are many rules regarding VA loans and they might not even be available in all areas. Still, ask if your bank or lending institution participates in the VA loan program.

Be forewarned, though. As a veteran, I have seen how stringent the VA requirements can be. As the Federal government gets deeper and deeper in debt, the Federal government will eventually stop backing home mortgages. The average taxpayer is not amused with the on-going scandals surrounding the Office of Veteran's Affairs. This can only translate into tighter requirements for all applicants.

Unfortunately, the tactics in this book may not work with the stringent requirements of most government-backed loans. There are limits on the dollar value of the house and the government will have their own appraisers (people who assign a monetary value to real estate).

Even though the Federal government will limit what you pay as a down payment, the government will probe into your financial background with a fine-tooth comb. If you have a mountain of debt, don't be too surprised if you are turned down for all of the VA loan programs. Even though all banks and lending institutions will look into your financial background, the Veteran's Affairs administration has the resources of the Federal government. If you have any debt, the Federal government will probably know about it. If you can't afford the down payment, the Federal government will know that, too. If you truly can't afford the down payment, apply for their "no down-payment" programs instead of using the tactics in this book.

In rural areas, the government has other loan programs. Like veterans, people in rural areas may need assistance in getting real estate loans from banks and lending institutions. Logically, rural areas will see less development. With less development, banks and lending institutions may not be eager to grant loans in these underdeveloped areas. Since property values are based on external demand, rural areas may not generate enough external demand. Without external demand, banks and lending institutions may not recoup their money if the borrower suddenly went into default. Thus, the Federal government may grant these banks and lending institutions a guarantee in case of borrower default.

Check with government websites first for low or no down-payment loan programs. Be sure to take advantage of any government programs, because you are a taxpayer. These are tax dollars at work for you. In truth, these government programs may be poorly advertised or not advertised at all. The ideas in this book allow you to borrow the necessary down-payment, but that may not be necessary if you can take advantage of a low or no down-payment loan program instead.

If you are not a veteran or you do not live in a rural area, continue to the next chapter. We will discuss borrowing the down-payment. When you borrow the down-payment, you will be using a concept called "leverage". Many people have used "leverage" to acquire riches. Even Donald Trump has used "leverage" many times in his fabled career. If used correctly, you can use "leverage" to your advantage, too.

I Bought My House with Credit Cards

LEVERAGE

When we use credit cards, we use borrowed money. When you borrow money, you are using leverage. According to Webster's Dictionary, the term leverage means "the use of credit to enhance one's speculative capacity".

Unfortunately, most people squander their leverage. Usually, people use credit cards to buy items they normally cannot afford. These include furniture, electronics, and other luxury items for the home that enhance their enjoyment and wrap them in comfort.

Wrongly, these people may see these luxury items as "investments". They may even have the mistaken impression of thinking that these items "appreciate" in value. Sadly, most electronic items such as computers, televisions, phones, and gadgets are usually outdated within eighteen months.

In truth, computers are outdated as soon as a new and improved model is presented to the public. Have you tried to sell a used computer lately? Have you noticed that your used computer does not even fetch half of the price you paid for it?

In the same way, phones become outdated. Used cellular phones are usually thrown away. Of course, some used cellular phones are given to charity. There are charitable organizations that re-program old cellular phones for battered women. Sadly though, the vast majority of cellular phones are rarely used again. Most of the time, it is cheaper to buy a new phone than to fix an old cellular phone made in the previous year.

Like electronics, our home furniture will rarely appreciate in value. True, salesmen will tell you that furniture are considered an "investment" item, but salesmen are trained to use the word "investment" instead of the word "cost". How do I know this? I have an audio book from the well-known sales trainer Tom Hopkins. In his audio book, Tom Hopkins instructs his students to substitute the fear-inducing word "cost" with the joy-inducing word "investment". Don't be fooled. If someone uses the word "investment" during a sales pitch, you can be certain that the item in question is not an "investment" at all.

In a similar way, used furniture appears on television shows like "Antiques Roadshow" and "Storage Wars", but used furniture that increases in value is the exception and not the rule. On these television shows, buyers look for furniture with a particular history. The buyers know where the furniture is manufactured and how they were designed. Usually, the furniture is from a bygone era. The antique furniture can even be centuries old.

Unfortunately for us, our mass-produced bedroom set won't be made by a famous designer. We would be lucky if the mattress was constructed to outlast the warranty. Most of us would be lucky if the bed frame survives the rigors of home life. I guarantee the kids will be jumping up and down on that bed as soon as you leave for vacation.

What about used furniture that is sold at garage sales and flea markets? Unfortunately, the owner receives just a small fraction of their money back (if any). If your furniture is made of pasteboard or particle board, you can be certain that no one wants to pay much for any of your furniture. Pasteboard and particle board is made of wood chips glued together. Exposure to moisture and heat expand and contract the wood chips. Over time, the wood will crack and splinter. After many years of use, pasteboard and particle board will lose its structural strength.

Have you tried selling a used mattress? I remember watching an old hotel being demolished next door. The demolition crew piled the used mattresses on the side of the road. To no one's surprise, no one wanted the used mattresses (much less pay for them). After reading all of this, I hope you will agree that furniture rarely qualifies as an "investment" item.

What *does* qualify as an investment? An investment is anything that appreciates in value. This includes stocks, bonds, precious metals, and real estate. Sadly, most consumers never use the leverage they have to buy anything that appreciates in value. These consumers have leverage in the form of that little piece of plastic in their wallet. Yes, we are talking about credit cards.

Sadly, millions of Americans have credit card debt they may never pay off. It is a billion-dollar industry that lures Americans with the promise of easy payment plans and low minimum payments. Instead of buying furniture, clothes, and electronics that eventually lose value, buy something that may appreciate in value. Buy yourself a home. Get yourself some real estate.

How can I buy a home with credit cards? If homes and real estate are such great investments, how come I can't just hand the seller my credit cards? That's a great question. Honestly, we buy everything else with credit cards. We pull up to the second window at the fast-food restaurant and hand them our credit card. We have people at the flea market who accept credit cards. We have churches that accept credit card payments. We can even pay our taxes with credit cards. Why not real estate?

I suspect the problem lies with the consumer lending industry. For example, I thought about buying stock with my credit cards. I went to my online broker's website. I looked carefully at all the ways I could pay. They take personal checks, but they don't take credit cards. I found that bizarre. We pay for everything else with credit cards. Why can't we buy stock with credit cards? I suspect the consumer lending industry does not want us to buy anything that appreciates in value over time. The credit card companies know that buying a cheeseburger won't make a consumer rich, but the credit card companies know that buying real estate and stock can make a consumer wealthy. As I looked closely at this, I noticed something peculiar. Fees take up the majority of money we pay to the credit card companies. If we pay only the minimum payment, the credit card companies hit us with fees and interest charges. The price of the cheeseburger eventually becomes the price of two cheeseburgers. I suspect the consumer lending industry is not here to make the consumer rich. In fact, the consumer lending industry is geared towards satisfying our need for instant gratification. The consumer lending industry is not here to help us find good investments.

I Bought My House with Credit Cards

According to Webster's Dictionary, the term investment means "the outlay of money usually for income or profit". In short, whatever money you spend brings back a return. Today, the term investment is thrown around by savvy sales people and Madison Avenue. As we said before, there are books on selling that instruct their readers to refer to their products as "investments" rather than luxury purchases.

In the 1990's, publishers of comic books were hawking special editions as "investments". These "special editions" were printed after news stories came out about superhero comic books from the thirties and forties. These old comic books were selling for six digits. Many collectors were giddy with excitement. Many people who had never read a comic book in their life purchased these special editions in the hope of easy money. Sadly, that easy money never materialized.

More than a hundred years ago, tulips were the hot commodity. In every generation, there is a craze that dominates the public. News stories about incredible rags-to-riches fables pumped up the demand for everything from Cabbage Patch dolls to deep fat turkey fryers. Turn on the television and watch the car auctions. Unless your car is in pristine condition with all the original parts, don't bother thinking that your automobile will garner more than what you paid for it. True, cars owned by celebrities can fetch some incredible prices. For most of us, our cars will usually end up at the junkyard as just one of the many piles of scrap metal.

Before the Great Recession of 2007-2009, there were many late-night television shows proclaiming that real estate was the way to riches. News outlets were running stories of people who sold their houses for twice to three times the price. Everywhere, people were trying to outbid everyone else. Every single acre of land that had a road seemed to be selling for astronomical prices. Real estate fever was everywhere. Was it the time to buy real estate? In hindsight, it was the wrong time to buy real estate. People who could not afford to pay their bills starting walking away from their homes. They mailed their keys to the bank and disappeared. As it turned out, many of these people had no jobs and no real way to pay the bank anyway.

What caused the Great Recession of 2007-2009? President Carter's 1977 Community Reinvestment Act made it law that banks should help all lenders regardless of location. In theory, the law was designed to remove all discrimination when it came to lending. In a perfect world, banks should use the same standards when evaluating potential borrowers. Eventually, the law was interpreted to mean that people in poor neighborhoods should be given the same opportunities to get loans as people in upscale neighborhoods. On paper, it was great idea. Over time, the banks relaxed their standards of underwriting so that they can meet the demands of the law. This gave birth to the sub-prime market. Sub-prime lenders were allowing people with less than stellar financial records to obtain loans. Since many banks did not want to carry these loans on their own books, these loans were repackaged to other people. When the sub-prime borrowers fell behind on their new mortgages, the defaulted loans had a devastating effect on many banks and underwriters. Like a string of dominoes, the lack of money returning to the banks caused many to close their doors forever. Ailing banks were sold to bigger banks that could absorb the losses. Eventually, all banks stopped lending. With no one borrowing money, the economy stopped expanding. People were laid off and the recession arrived.

I Bought My House with Credit Cards

SHOULD I BUY REAL ESTATE?

Before you jump into real estate, there are many reasons to be cautious. Like any major purchase, you will probably need a loan. Sure, you can let your home go into foreclosure, but you won't be saving any money on insurance and interest rates in the future. This could translate into thousands of dollars in additional costs for you and your family.

Before you jump into real estate, let us discuss the major reasons why you should wait first. Real estate is not for everyone. Here are a few things to think about:

The first big reason to think twice about buying real estate is because everyone else is doing it. If people are bidding up the prices of the homes in your neighborhood, don't be caught up in the excitement. In these situations, you need to be the seller. There is an old saying that the best place to be in a bidding war is on the losing side. Indeed, this was the case before the Great Recession of 2007-2009. There were record prices being paid for homes in Las Vegas and Phoenix. Many cities saw greatly inflated prices for real estate. Everywhere you turned, someone was making big money selling their house.

Here is a story from my own personal experience. My next-door neighbor was selling his modest one thousand square foot home. Miraculously, his home sold in less than ten days. Encouraged by the quick sale, I decided to sell our own house. To my detriment, I took my time getting the house ready. I postponed everything until spring. I thought my house would have a better chance to sell in the springtime. As luck would have it, the world had changed overnight. I waited too long to put the house on the market. By the time we had prepared the house to be shown, no one wanted to buy. One after another, banks were closing their doors forever. These banks had bad loans on their books. Each time I watched television, I was bombarded by bad news. I had lost my golden opportunity. I thought everyone was getting into real estate. Thus, I thought there would be plenty of buyers for my house. I was sadly mistaken.

What lesson did I learn? If people are bidding up the prices of real estate, do not buy. By all means, sell any real estate that you have if there are people buying. In the same way, wait until the boom is over and you can probably get a great deal on whatever you want to buy.

The second big reason to think twice about buying real estate is quite obvious. Is there more than one foreclosed home in your neighborhood? You might consider staying out of the real estate game until the economy improves. If all of your neighbors are packing up and leaving, don't bother jumping into the real estate market. If you see one news story after another about a bad real estate market, don't be the last one to heed the warnings. If you see more than one moving van in your neighborhood, be sure to investigate. Are they moving in or are they moving out? If the people are loading the mattresses into the truck, you can be sure that these people are leaving your neighborhood.

I Bought My House with Credit Cards

When there are lots of foreclosures, it is very difficult to get an accurate appraisal. Foreclosures are homes that are usually sold at deep discounts. To get a price on a house, a bank or lending institution will send an appraiser. *(An appraiser is real estate professional that determines the price of real estate.)* When an appraiser sees the prices of the foreclosed properties, the appraiser will use the lower prices of the foreclosed properties. If the bank sees a lower-than-average price for your home, the bank may not want to use that lower-than-average price for your home. In some cases, the bank may see that you owe more to the bank than this lower-than-average price for your home. This means the bank is obligated not to charge you private mortgage insurance. In some cases, the bank cannot get you a home equity line of credit because of this lower-than-average price for your home. In these cases, the bank may just throw out this lower-than-average price for your home. This means you cannot refinance your home or get a home equity line of credit.

As we have seen, the price of real estate is based on many factors. Usually, appraisers choose at least three similar properties in the vicinity. In an economic downturn, any one of the three properties may be a foreclosure. As a rule, most banks do not advertise foreclosed properties. As a result, the appraiser may not know the deeply discounted house is actually a foreclosed property. He or she has no way of knowing for sure. As a result, the price could be skewed towards the deeply discounted house. This might be good if you are buying, but this is not good if you are trying to sell. If the price is too low for the seller, the appraiser may not finish the appraisal at all. The appraiser might not even finish the appraisal due to a "lack of adequate information". This actually happened to me when I tried to refinance my house. Since the appraiser could not get an accurate price on my house, the bank decided not to refinance my house. There were too many foreclosures in our neighborhood. In most cases, the lack of a professional appraisal stops the refinancing process entirely.

The third big reason to think twice about buying real estate is your own bad credit. Let's be honest. If you have good credit, you probably would not be reading this book. You may want to get an even bigger house and that's a perfectly legitimate reason to be reading this book.

However, all is not lost. There is a way back from the abyss. As the author of this book, I am living proof of this. My first wife spent money like water. In my short first marriage, she accumulated $30,000.00 in credit card debt. Luckily, I had the good sense to go to a non-profit credit counseling service. *(Don't ever use a for-profit credit counseling service.)* These wonderful people contacted my creditors. They had the late fees waived. They arranged for me to pay back only the principal. Each month, I would drop off a thousand dollar check. The credit counseling service did the rest. After six years, I paid back every dime I owed.

If that was not bad enough, my second wife had $40,000.00 of her own credit card debt. I will chronicle later how I bounced back from this. Fortunately for you, I will detail a few tactics I learned along the way. If you really want to erase your all of your debt, read Kevin Trudeau's <u>Debt</u>

I Bought My House with Credit Cards

Cures™ "They" Don't Want You to Know.

The fourth big reason to think twice about jumping into real estate is your high debt ratio. Let's be realistic. The bank or lending institution will want to know if you can fulfill all of your financial obligations. One way that banks or lending institutions determine your ability to pay is to calculate your debt ratio. Your debt ratio is simply your monthly financial obligations divided by your monthly take-home pay. Your debt ratio is normally expressed as a percent.

If your bills exceed more than half of your income, it is doubtful you can even get a bank to finance your new home. In the fact, the maximum debt ratio was 42% before the Great Recession of 2007-2009. Today, the maximum debt ratio is probably no more than 38%. The bank or lending institution should tell you the maximum debt ratio they would accept prior to approving a loan.

The monthly financial obligations include all car payments, all student loans, and the minimum payments on all of your credit cards. Be sure to include all consumer lines of credit, because most of them will show up on your credit report. Gas cards and cards from major retailers may not show up on your credit card, but you should include these in your calculations anyway. If you happen to skip a few (or fail to show one or more of the larger payments), you can be sure that your loan will be rejected. Your loan officer may think that you are not being completely truthful. If your loan officer starts to doubt your credibility in one area, you can be sure they will look over the rest of your application with a magnifying lens.

Your bank or lending institution will ask you to fill out a "List of Financial Obligations" as part of your application. Be sure to have addresses and phone numbers to all of your creditors. Be warned that credit reports are not perfect. If you have a zero balance on any credit card, please be sure to check your credit report to see if this was updated. There is nothing worse than paying off a credit card and finding out that your credit report still shows a balance.

The bank or lending institution will add the proposed mortgage payment (with taxes and insurance) to your current monthly obligations. Of course, the rent payment will not be included. The bank or lending institution will assume you will be moving into your new house. If you are getting a vacation home or you are purchasing a rental home, make sure your monthly income will cover the added mortgage payment.

If your debt ratio is still acceptable, the bank or lending institution usually goes ahead with the loan. Oftentimes, the bank or lending institution will ask for additional information. Don't panic. Try to answer their questions in a timely and accurate manner. If you appear nervous, the loan officer may continue to ask more questions until he or she is satisfied you can re-pay the loan. Remember, the loan officer's job is dependent on making solid loans that will be paid on time. Banks and lending institutions do not make money on foreclosures.

Be forewarned. Some banks and lending institutions may have different ways of calculating debt ratio. In fact, the loan officer may "assign" nominal balances to one or all of your zero balance credit cards. This means, the bank or lending institution will see if you can still meet all of your monthly financial obligations (even if recent credit card transactions were not reported). Yes, banks and lending institutions know that you can still be using your credit cards even after they check your credit report.

Be sure none of your credit cards have reached their credit limit. In fact, make sure the balances are less than half of the credit limit. A credit card at the maximum credit limit is a red flag to all loan officers. If you have more than one credit card at their credit limit, don't be surprised if the loan officer stops the loan process. Make sure all of your credit card balances are less than half of their maximum limit and verify that this is shown on your credit report.

If your credit card balances are greater, the loan officer may stop the loan process. If this happens, don't panic. Put this book back on the shelf and take a year or so to reduce your credit card debt. Of course, you might have to do a lifestyle change. I know I did.

How do you make a lifestyle change to take control of your credit card purchases? Use cash. I know that sounds simple, but it *does* work. For me, I used a set amount of cash each month and paid everything else with a check. I used no credit cards at all. In fact, I took half of my pay for rent and credit card balances. Everything else was paid by cash or check. Since writing a check at the grocery store was a hassle, I had to watch my cash very carefully. I also used cash at the gas station. Over time, I stopped all unnecessary trips to save on gas money. I stopped buying junk food and candy. I had to plan all of my meals so my cash would not run out. I cut coupons. I stopped seeing people who only wanted to party. In fact, I left the party crowd because I had to get a second job. When I wasn't working, I was sleeping.

Did the lifestyle change work? Yes. As an added bonus, I also discovered my true friends. These were people who really cared about me. They wanted to help me during my crisis. They did not look down on me because I used coupons. They did not mock me because I could no longer buy all the newest gadgets and gizmos. Like me, you will soon discover your true friends when you make this lifestyle change. Don't be too surprised that you have a lot of friends that just want you to spend money on *them*. When your money runs out, they will run away from *you*, too.

Once you get your credit card balances under control, you can go back to the loan process with much more confidence. Who knows? You might even be approved for the loan this time.

What if I don't agree with the bank's assessment of my credit report? Truthfully, there is not much you can do once they reject your application. Remember, there are no standardized guidelines for calculating your debt ratio. Your best course of action is to lower your credit card balances.

Before you even see a loan officer, calculate for yourself your own debt ratio. Can you really make the monthly payments? If not, you can always look for real estate that is less expensive. If necessary, put this book on the shelf until your debt ratio is more manageable.

Sure, some lenders who do not care about your high debt ratio, but your interest rate will be very high. The monthly payment alone may make the loan unaffordable. As we said before, be sure to calculate your debt ratio before you fill out the application at the bank. If your debt ratio is too high, work on paying off the highest interest credit cards first. Hold off on buying a new car and cut back on the expensive vacations. The name of the game is to lower your monthly bills before asking for the loan. As always, check your credit report every time you reach a zero balance on any of your financial obligations. What's the use in paying off your financial obligations if they never show up on your credit report?

The fifth big reason to think twice about jumping into real estate is cheap rent. If you're living in your mother's basement, you might consider saving up a year's worth of money before embarking on the quest for real estate. Try looking online for a house you would really like to get. Find the asking price for that house. Go to the website of your favorite bank and get their interest rate for a home loan. If it is not on their website, make a phone call. They are usually happy to tell you. Calculate the monthly mortgage payment. There are simple online tools nowadays that can automatically calculate your monthly mortgage payment. Just plug in the price of the home and the bank interest rate. If the proposed monthly mortgage payment is double the amount of rent you pay (or more), I recommend waiting and saving a year's worth of cash first. You might even choose a less expensive house. Once more, go online and calculate the projected monthly payment. If the monthly payment is not any closer to your monthly payments, wait and save your money. Remember, you must have enough cash for the many out-of-pocket expenses like appraisals that will eat up your cash.

The sixth big reason to think twice about jumping into real estate is your lack of job security. If you hear that there will be layoffs, do not attempt to buy any real estate. I remember how my father was laid off one day before closing. If there were any early warnings, my father did not see them. In fact, most people never know until they lose their job. The security guard escorts them to the front door with a box of their personal belongings.

What should I do? Keep abreast of what is happening in business. Even a cursory glance at the business section in the paper will reveal clues to the long-term health of companies in your city. Find out if your employer is going through re-structuring. Usually re-structuring goes hand-in-hand with downsizing.

Does your employer carry a lot of debt? Is your employer about to be bought by a conglomerate or even a competitor? You should pay attention to any of these warning signs. If everyone is just sitting around idle, the company will probably cut back on staffing. If everyone is scratching their heads about the lack of sales, the management staff is probably scratching their heads looking for ways to cut back on the number of employees.

Your job is the key to buying real estate. Without a steady job, most banks and lending institutions will not approve a loan. Historically, banks and lending institutions did approve loans for people without steady jobs, but that was before the Great Recession of 2007-2009. If you want to be successful, having a job and keeping a job is one of the most important parts of getting into real estate. Even if you get rental income from real estate, the cash received may not be able to replace your income completely. You might have to work a while before that happens.

Perhaps, your line of work is the real problem. Are you in an industry that does not have a future? Your company might not have such a bright future if it only makes typewriters. What about companies manufacturing pagers, PDAs, public payphones, video-cassette-recorders, fax machines, maps, phone books, encyclopedias, and floppy disks? What if you work in a video rental store? An industry that makes out-dated technology will eventually cease to exist.

The seventh big reason to think twice about jumping into real estate is because you like to move from place to place. In the first thirty years of my life, I have had thirty different home addresses. My father loved to move every eighteen months. As a result, I do not have a lot of childhood friends because I never had time to cultivate any long-term friendships. As an adult, I moved from place to place wherever the Navy would send me. Once I entered the corporate world, I still insisted on moving wherever there was employment. To no one's surprise, I was not approved for a home loan until I had stable employment and one address.

Sure, there is nothing wrong with moving from place to place. However, the bank may question the reasons about each move. These questions may lead to other questions. Did you move because you were changing jobs? Was there a reason why you moved all the way from New York to California? If your job is so steady, why did the company move you three times in the last ten years? You may not want to tell the bank the real reasons why you moved.

Sure, a beachfront property in Alaska is not like a beachfront property in Florida. The bank may understand why you moved to the beaches of Florida, but the bank may not understand why you moved to the beaches of Alaska. Sure, you can build the same kind of house in these different locations, but the bank may ask why you want to build a beach house in Alaska.

There are costs associated with real estate that renters do not worry about. You can waste a great deal of money buying and selling houses every few years. It is even harder to get a home equity line of credit. The home equity line of credit is based on the difference between the appraised value of the home and the amount remaining on the mortgage loan. Theoretically, the amount you can borrow against the equity of your house increases the longer you stay in a home.

The eighth big reason to think twice about jumping into real estate is because your job requires you to travel a great deal. Traveling salesmen, corporate negotiators, business consultants, truck drivers, and military personnel are required to move from place to place. Unfortunately, real estate is never portable. Besides, someone needs to be in your home so vandals and vagrants are not attracted to your empty house.

In this case, you are better off renting. The added costs *(of buying and selling a home)* are hard to recoup. Different regions of the country have different costs of living. The cost of an apartment in

Manhattan might be as expensive as a mansion along the bayou.

Still, there are great ideas in this book. You can use the ideas in this book to buy real estate in more than one location as rental properties. If you've ever wanted to be a landlord, you can get started with this book. If your job requires you to travel, why not have rental properties wherever you visit?

The ninth big reason to think twice about jumping into real estate is your propensity to jump from one relationship to the next. This is similar to having a job that requires you to travel a great deal.

In an ideal world, banks and lending institutions would not look at a person's marital status when assessing a person's creditworthiness. For example, a divorce can prompt a sale of the couple's domicile. Sure, the loan is usually paid off when the home is sold. Any profit is split between the two parties. In a bad economy, this may not be the case. In fact, some homes may go into foreclosure because neither party wants to pay the monthly mortgage. The bank may go to court, but there is no guarantee the bank will get any money from either party.

In the same way, the bank or lending institution may not want to know about your long-distance relationship. The bank or lending institution wants to know if you will pay your monthly mortgage payment on time. They might not be so happy if you tell them that you would consider moving to wherever your lover wants to go.

The tenth big reason to think twice about jumping head first into real estate is the down payment. Simply put, the down payment is the percentage of the asking price that a bank wants before they give you a loan. Most mortgage lenders ask for 5% to 10% of the asking price, but they would prefer that you make a down payment of 20%. With a 20% down payment, the bank or lending institution gets more of their money before you even make the first mortgage payment. In fact, most of the first mortgage payment goes to the interest being charged. Not much of the first mortgage payment goes towards the principle. This is pure profit for the bank or lending institution. Just in case the lender defaults on the loan, the bank or lending institution can draw from this "profit" to pay for foreclosure proceedings. The loan officer knows the bank or lending institution will lose money on any foreclosure, so the mortgage payments are specifically designed to pull as much "profit" at the beginning of the loan period.

Fortunately for you, this book will teach you how to "borrow" that down payment from your credit cards. Of course, you may not be able to "borrow" enough for a 20% down payment, but you may be able to "borrow" enough for a 5% or 10% down payment.

I Bought My House with Credit Cards

WHERE SHOULD I BUY?

Where should I buy land? The trick is to see where people are living and where they will ultimately build new structures. Look around. Where are those cement trucks going? If you have to ask, call up anyone that you know in the construction business. I call this the "following the cement truck" method of determining where to buy land. Since concrete is used to build everything from bridges to basements, you will quickly find out where they are building. Take your map and find the locations where new structures and roads are being built. You will soon discover the direction of new construction. Probably, you can pick up real estate bargains along the direction of this new construction. This will guarantee that your parcel of land will become increasing valuable.

For me, I discovered that our city was constructing a loop on the outer edges of town. At the time, there were little or no buildings beside the roads that were being built. After searching on the internet, I found a home builder that had purchased an undeveloped tract of land near this massive road project. To no one's surprise, new commercial developments popped up near this massive road project. Years later, an outlet mall was built near my new house. Slowly, the price of our house started to creep higher. I am sure our modest house will continue to increase in value as more structures are built nearby.

On the other hand, I would not buy a parcel of land in a blighted neighborhood. If there are people loitering around, you can be sure the unemployment rate is higher on that part of town. If there is more than one car with missing tires, you can be certain the residents know who has the missing tires. If more than one car is on cinder blocks, you may need to walk a little bit faster. You don't want to be the victim of a crime. Are the windows are covered with plywood? People usually put plywood over the windows when there are reports of hurricanes or tornados in the vicinity. Is there more graffiti than street signs? Is trash blowing around freely on the streets? There's a good chance this is a blighted neighborhood.

A blighted neighborhood will not be a safe place to be at night. Look at the light levels where you want to buy property. Check if there is a lack of illumination along sidewalks. Ask the neighbors if they are afraid to walk around at night. Don't be afraid to ask. If you really are afraid to ask, I strongly suggest you take your search for real estate to another location.

Remember, it is much easier to fix a house than it is to fix a neighborhood. Sometimes, good people stay in a bad neighborhood only because they can't sell their property right away. The local economy may have changed. A large employer may have disappeared. All of a sudden, no one wants to buy their house. Usually, the elderly will hide in their homes because the youths have all turned to crime.

Keep in mind that you are looking for safe place for someone to live. That someone might just be you. Don't be lured by inexpensive property in bad neighborhoods. It is inexpensive for a reason. Be warned that it is very hard to sell property in a blighted neighborhood.

I Bought My House with Credit Cards

WHERE ARE YOUR PAPERS?

Before you get started, you must get your financial information together. The bank or lending institution may send you a list. By all means, follow the list.

First and foremost, you must have identification. This includes a driver's license or photo identification. Know your social security number. If you don't have a social security number, bring your naturalization number. If you are an illegal alien, stop the process here. Remember, all real estate transactions are public record. There's no need to tell the world that you are here illegally.

Next, search out all of your paystubs for your current employment. If you don't have paid employment, the bank or lending institution will not lend you money. Let's face it. With no current job, you will not have the means to pay the bank their monthly mortgage. Sure, there have been lending institutions who have given loans to unemployed people before the Great Recession of 2007-2009, but they are probably not in business anymore. No doubt, they declared bankruptcy or they were sold to larger banks and lending institutions.

As we have said before, your career is the key to real estate. Steady employment is always welcome. Sure, some lending institutions have treated child support, alimony payments, and disability payments as income when making loan calculations before the Great Recession of 2007-2009. Alas, these lending institutions have discovered that deadbeat dads may forget to pay child support. The ex-husband might move to another state and skip out on the alimony payments. The government may stop paying disability payments because their neighbor saw them mowing their lawn. In short, the bank and lending institution sees a solid job as essential in paying them back. Let's face it. Despite what the politicians may say, banks and lending institutions are in business only because they make a profit. If they don't, they won't be open for long.

After that, get your tax returns. Get full five years worth of tax returns. If you are above the age of consent with no tax returns, you might not even be considered for a loan unless you can come up with a 20% to 33% down payment. If you don't have any tax returns, you might need to work a few years first. You can always partner with a family member for your first purchase, but most adults may not be willing to be a co-signer for a loan.

Start by calling up your own bank that has your checking account. If you already have a checking or savings account with a bank or lending institution, you are one step closer to that mortgage. Why? The bank or lending institution can simply pull up your open accounts. They will immediately see spending and saving patterns. If they see that you are keeping more of your money in their savings account, they are more apt to lend you money.

What if I don't have a checking account? Open a checking account right away. Try credit unions first. Your employer may already be part of a network of credit unions, so it does not hurt to ask the human resources department of your employer. Even if you employer is associated with a large bank, you might save a few dollars on transactions fees and other charges. Always ask the bank about their fees. Sometimes, these are published on their website. Check if they make home loans. If they don't, find a bank or credit union that does home loans. Historically, credit unions charge less than regular banks. Credit unions have enjoyed renewed popularity after the Great Recession of 2007-2009. Many people became disillusioned at the lackluster service they received from the large banks. Their onerous fees sent people in droves to the doors of credit unions.

Once you open up a checking account, open up a savings account, too. Throw all of your extra cash into this saving account. True, savings accounts give only a pittance when it comes to interest. That is not the goal here. What you want to do is show the bank or credit union that you like to save money. Remember, loan officers want to see that you have money. They want to see that you are disciplined about money.

What next? Don't be too surprised if the bank or credit union sends you an advertisement from their loan department. The advertisement may have their published rates and a phone number. Call the phone number. Be blunt. Ask if you even qualify for any of their loans. You might be pleasantly surprised. Sometimes, there are special programs for fire-fighters, teachers, police officers, and other government workers. Don't be afraid to ask if there are certain builders that meet their loan criteria. Most important of all, ask what it would take to qualify for any of their loans.

How long do I need to be in the workforce to qualify for a loan? How long do I need to be at my current job to qualify for a loan? What information do you need to make a loan? How much do I have to have in my checking account? Of course, the loan officer may ask you to schedule an appointment. Bring whatever information the loan officer needs to make an accurate assessment.

Expect all lenders to ask where you work and how long. Have the name of your supervisor ready with his or her contact information. Usually, the loan officer will want a daytime telephone number. Have all your paystubs ready. If the pay is not steady, give the loan officer the normal amount of hours you work in a week. If you have a sales job, have written records showing them how often and in what amounts you were paid. Give the loan officer the date you were hired.

If you are self-employed, the loan officer will want more information. If you have a C Corporation or Limited Liability Corporation, provide tax identification numbers and financial records. Usually, C Corporations and Limited Liability Corporations require tax preparation by an accountant. Bring all of the corporate or LLC tax information. Your C Corporation or Limited Liability Corporation may be less than three years old. In this case, you might need to provide receipts and contracts. In short, you need to prove to the loan officer that you have the means to pay back the loan.

The loan officer will want to see your car payment book. If the car loan is paid off, the loan officer may want to see the title to the car. This information should appear on your credit report, but there could be erroneous information. The lending institution will usually mail you the car title once the car loan is paid off. Of course, bring all your latest credit card statements. Indeed, this information is readily available to the loan officer through the credit report, but at this point in time, the loan officer has not pulled up your credit report.

If you already have a mortgage on an existing home, the loan officer will want to know all about your current home. Bring the payment book and all of the mortgage information you can find. The loan officer will want to know if have skipped any payments or made any late payments. If there are second mortgages or home equity lines of credit on your current home, bring all the documentation on that. Be forewarned that the loan officer may immediately turn you down if they see more than one financial obligation tied to each property. Even if they did approve you for a loan, you will not get the best interest rate. Re-calculate the proposed monthly mortgage to reflect the higher interest rate. If the proposed monthly payment is too much, stop the loan process now. I recommend paying off the second mortgage and closing the home equity line of credit on your current home, first. One single house payment is best. When you get to that point, you can restart the loan process.

Please note that you might not be buying a house in which to live. You might be buying a vacation home. Lenders will have different rules for second homes. Of course, you might want a second home to rent out. Lenders have different rules for rental homes, too. In fact, many lenders may even shy away from these purchases. If this is the case, stop now. Don't go any further with the loan process with this particular bank or lending institution. Next time, ask if the bank or credit union even makes loans for investment property.

LOANS, LOANS, LOANS

Do people purchase real estate with cash?

Sure, there have been people who have bought real estate with cash. Usually, these are people who have won the lottery or received an inheritance from a generous family member. In most situations, that amount of cash will certainly attract the attention of law enforcement and the taxing authorities. Even people who have won money in game shows have been forced to give up the appropriate amount of money to pay taxes. Afterwards, these municipalities take an additional percentage at the end of the year from the increased income.

True, there have been stories of drug dealers buying real estate with cash. Since the sale of real estate is part of the public record, these stories are few and far between. The last thing drug dealers want to do is to have their name as part of any public record. More often than not, criminals find law-abiding citizens who will gladly purchase property for them in exchange for a hefty bonus. Thus, the criminal's name is never part of any legal document.

Be advised that there are many types of loans for real estate. This is because there are many types of real estate. A bank or lending institution may tailor a loan for an undeveloped parcel of land differently than a home equity line of credit on an existing house in an old subdivision. There can also be more than one loan on a piece of property with different payment schedules and interest rates.

Usually, consumers get a fixed-rate mortgage. Normally, these fixed-rate mortgages are for 15 year or 30 year periods. Lately, the consumer lending industry is tossing around the idea of 40 and 50 year fixed-rate mortgages. These fixed-rate mortgages are widely accepted, because the monthly payments do not change. This gives the consumer great confidence that their payments never go up despite the fluctuations of the market interest rates. Since the payments never change, banks and lending institutions can more accurately project their future profits. Thus, banks and lending institutions offer better interest rates. With better interest rates, the fixed-rate mortgage becomes very affordable.

Fixed-rate mortgages made over a 30 year period are generally lower because they are amortized over a longer period of time. This allows consumers to put their excess cash into more profitable investments that are riskier. No doubt, the 30 year fixed-rate mortgage charges more interest over the long–term versus the 15 year fixed–rate mortgage. Still, the higher interest charged means more deductions are tax time. This has the effect of lowering taxes for those with 30 year fixed-rate mortgages. The consumer can pay off debt, invest the difference, or simply spend the tax savings. Still, the consumer acquires little to no equity in the first few years. It may be harder to borrow if one has a 30 year fixed-rate mortgage versus a comparable 15 year fixed–rate mortgage.

In contrast, a fixed-rate mortgage made over a 15 year period allows the consumer to accumulate more equity than a comparable 30 year fixed rate mortgage. The monthly payments are so much higher for that same reason. Don't be too surprised when you might have to settle for a smaller house because of the higher monthly payments.

What is an assumable loan? An assumable loan is usually a fixed-rate loan in which anyone can take over the loan payments. Most assumable loans were made a long time ago when most home loans were FHA and VA approved. Thus, these assumable loans are typically very affordable. Unfortunately, these assumable loans are harder and harder to find. Nowadays, most banks and lending institutions shy away from assumable loans. At the present time, banks and lending institutions want to know and see who is borrowing their money. Gone are the days when a promise was sealed with a handshake.

Now, let us look a different type of loan. According to Bruce Harwood's Real Estate Principles, an adjustable rate mortgage (ARM) is "a mortgage loan on which the interest rate rises and falls with changes in prevailing rates". These adjustable rate mortgages are tied to widely-published market indexes. As the market index goes up and down, your mortgage rate fluctuates up and down with the market index. If you plan to move in less than five years, it may be advantageous to get an adjustable rate mortgage with a low introductory interest rate. At times, the low introductory interest rate may last for the first two to three years (or more) before it is adjusted up or down.

There are different types of adjustable rate mortgages. The introductory "teaser" rate may last anywhere from one month to one decade. No doubt, the bank or lending institution is betting that interest rates go up. In the beginning, the most fashionable adjustable rate mortgage had a full year of the low introductory rate. Soon afterwards, the 5/1 ARM came into prominence. The 5/1 ARM had five years of introductory interest rates. Subsequently, the adjustable rate mortgage adjusts every year afterwards until the loan is paid.

There are also other adjustable rate mortgages where the period of adjustment is more than one year. These adjustable rate mortgages are called "hybrids" because they start resembling fixed-rate mortgages. The consumer is assured that their interest rate will not rise for an extended period of time. The consumer has some time to shop around for a better mortgage if market index starts to rise. Personally, I have discovered that some builders will try to lure customers from other builders by offering these low introductory interest rates. Usually, these are builders who are trying to break into a particular market. For me, I was given a low introductory interest rate. The rate would not change for the first few years. This gave me time to pay off the cash advance I used as a down payment. After the introductory interest rates went away, I re-financed the house to a regular 30 year fixed rate mortgage.

If you decide on the adjustable rate mortgage, make sure you understand how and when your mortgage will move up and down. Sometimes, there is a maximum percentage rate that the ARM can jump and a maximum percentage rate that the ARM can jump down. Usually there is also a minimum percentage rate and a maximum percentage rate, but you have to check the fine print.

I Bought My House with Credit Cards

The bank or lending institution may not readily publish any information on the maximum or minimum interest rate. Don't be too surprised if your adjustable rate mortgage jumps faster and higher than expected. That new interest rate could make your monthly payment completely unreasonable.

These adjustable rate mortgages can be tied to the yield on the one-year Treasury bill. (You can get this information from the Federal Reserve Board's website.) These adjustable rate mortgages can also be tied to interest rates paid to depositors, namely the COFI. The COFI (11th District Cost of Funds) tracks how much interest is paid on bank deposits in the western states. Finally, adjustable rate mortgages can be tied to the London Interbank Offered Rate (LIBOR). The LIBOR rate tracks the fees of large international banks for outsized loans.

What is a "conforming" loan?

President Carter's 1977 Community Reinvestment Act paved the way for millions to get access to home loans. In this way, the United States government became entrenched in the housing industry. Like most governmental agencies, rules were created to streamline the loan process. Thus, the "conforming loan" was born. The Federal government determined the prices of homes they can guarantee. In other words, certain government agencies (affectionately called Fannie Mae and Freddie Mac) were created. These agencies would back up these mortgages for these homeowners up to a certain amount.

The limits to "conforming" loans are set based on the price of houses from October of last year to October of the current year. In 2008, legislation designated areas where housing costs are much higher. Notwithstanding, these areas are designated "high-cost" areas. The limits for "conforming" loans in these areas are much higher.

When a loan becomes a "conforming" loan, your mortgage may be sent to another bank or lending institution. This new bank or lending institution will "service" your mortgage. In other words, the new bank or lending institution will accept your mortgage payments. Eventually, they will provide you with the title to the land when the mortgage is paid off. The bank or lending institution that initially made the "conforming" loan with you has "sold" the loan to that new bank or lending institution. That means the bank or lending institution that made the loan with you will receive a fee. The new bank or lending institution will recoup the cost of fee with the interest payments that are included with your mortgage.

Before the Great Recession of 2007-2009, many of these "conforming" loans were re-packaged as "mortgage-backed securities". Since some of these "conforming" loans were made to people who really could not afford these loans, many of the banks and lending institutions that made these loans did not want to keep these "high-risk" loans on the books. As the "high-risk" loans defaulted, the investors who bought these "mortgage-backed securities" lost billions of dollars.

With all of the requirements necessary to get a "conforming" loan, why were these "conforming" loans "high-risk" loans? There were lending institutions that did not verify employment records. Some lending institutions purposely falsified information to make the homebuyer appear more "credit-worthy". Subsequently, the people in charge of these lending institutions were prosecuted. Today, the Federal government charges an extra quarter to half of a percent of the home price when "conforming" loans are transferred from one lending institution to another. The idea is to keep lending institutions from making "high-risk" loans in the first place, especially if the lending institution knows that the "high-risk" loan cannot immediately be transferred. In short, the lending institution that originated the loan is held responsible for the quality of the loan.

To add to the confusion, many banks were being pressured to fulfill loans in less-than-desirable locations per the 1977 Community Reinvestment Act. To appear "socially responsible", these banks succumbed to political pressure and made the "high-risk" loans. These were the same banks and lending institutions that eventually failed. In the Great Recession of 2007-2009, these banks were sold to bigger banks to prevent the collapse of the United States banking system.

Most Americans do not realize the influence of the Federal government on the banking industry. Since the banks do business with the Federal Reserve on a daily basis, any shift in Federal policy has monumental significance. It is no surprise that private lenders eventually changed their own home loans so that they mimicked the government standard. In this way, the private lenders could take advantage of these government programs if necessary.

Nowadays, Fannie Mac and Freddie Mac limit conforming loans to less than half a million for a single-family house (except in Alaska and Hawaii). In 2010, the limit for a conforming loan in Alaska, Hawaii, Guam, and the U.S. Virgin Islands was set higher than the half million dollar mark. Part of what these government-sponsored agencies do is to determine how large a "conforming" loan can be. They also control the maximum debt-to-income ratio, minimum credit score, recommended credit history, list of required documents, and the maximum amount of the down payment.

Of course, there were different dollar amounts for the home loans depending on the region. These dollar amounts were adjusted at regular intervals. The Office of Federal Housing Enterprise Oversight (OFHEO) made sure that Fannie Mae (Federal National Mortgage Association, started in 1968) and Freddie Mac (Federal Home Loan Mortgage Corporation, started in 1970) were adequately funded in case any of the borrowers failed to meet their financial obligation. This same agency was responsible for publishing average housing prices for each region of the country. In 2008, the Housing and Economic Recovery Act of 2008 put the Office of Federal Housing Enterprise Oversight and the Federal Housing Finance Board (FHFB) under the newly created Federal Housing Finance Agency (FHFA).

Be forewarned. Many home builders may not even qualify for government-backed loans, because most builders are there to make a profit. Many home builders put a premium on their lots, but the government will not back any loans for overpriced real estate.

Expect a conventional loan to ask for a minimum of 10% down payment. In other words, a $100,000.00 home will require a down payment of $10,000.00. Of course, the bank wants you to put down more, preferably a 20% down payment. That's a whopping $20,000.00 on a $100,000.00 home. Of course, banks give you the best interest rate only if you put down at least 20% for the down payment.

In some cases, a bank will even waive their PMI (private mortgage insurance) if you put down at least a third of the asking price. In today's market, most home loans will include PMI. I suspect private mortgage insurance is a surcharge that banks use to cover foreclosure expenses when someone defaults on their loan. When a loan balance reaches 78% of the original value of the home, the PMI is required by law to go away. Usually banks or lending institutions don't tell you when this happens. Sadly, most people continue paying PMI long after the PMI was scheduled to go away. These extra payments are just additional profits to the bank, so banks and lending institutions don't volunteer this information.

A loan that is larger than the "conforming" loan is called a "jumbo" loan. Your bank or lending institution may not even support "jumbo" loans. Don't be too surprised with the endless documentation requirements for a jumbo loan. With a conforming loan, Fannie Mae has been dictating the required documentation and loan limits since 1970. With a jumbo loan, the individual bank or lending institution dictates the required documentation and loan limits. Suddenly, you might not qualify to a get a loan at all because of the stringent requirements. Let's face it. Jumbo loans are not commonplace, especially with a sluggish economy. Banks and lending institutions may not readily want to assume the added risk of a jumbo loan.

Jumbo loans are usually for high-earners. High-earners usually want more expensive homes. The price tags on these expensive homes may easily exceed the limits of "conforming" loans. Usually these high-earners are self-employed and/or business owners. Naturally, banks and lending institutions will need more documentation to see the entire financial health of an individual who wants to borrow. This includes a minimum credit score of 660, possibly 720 or higher (to get a better interest rate). Two years after the Great Recession of 2007-2009, the interest rates were between 5½ to 6½ percent. Compare that to roughly 4½ percent for a "conforming loan" during the same time period. Do not be surprised if the lender asks for a 20% down payment. Expect a higher interest rate if you want to give only a 10% down payment.

I do not recommend asking for a jumbo loan. There is no need to attract unnecessary attention from the bank and lending institution. In fact, the documentation requirements of a jumbo loan may reveal your financial health more completely to the bank and lending institution. Since we are trying to borrow the down payment, you can be certain that the bank and lending institution will uncover this.

I Bought My House with Credit Cards

The last loan I want to talk about is an "interest-only" loan. Unlike all other loans, no part of the payment is ever used to pay down the principal. The principal is just a legal word to define the amount borrowed from the bank or lending institution. At the end of the loan period, the borrower does not get the title to the property at all. Either the bank sells the property or the bank receives a huge balloon payment from the borrower. Neither scenario is a good outcome for the borrower.

What is a balloon payment? A balloon payment is a lump-sum payment that exceeds the normal monthly payment on a loan. The balloon payment may occur at regular intervals or at the very end of the loan period.

Before the stock market crash of 1929, loans with balloon payments were commonplace. Unfortunately, many people did not have the means to fund the balloon payments. Many declared bankruptcy or left town. Banks closed their doors permanently when people started defaulting on their loans. When the banks closed their doors, there was panic in the streets. No one was loaning any money any more. People started to withdraw all of their money from the banks that were still open. With no money in circulation, businesses started closing their doors, too. This was the start of the Great Depression.

Why would anyone agree to a loan that has "balloon" payments? I suspect that the monthly payments are probably very reasonable. Since no part of the monthly payment would go towards the principal, the monthly payment would be much lower. I suspect these loans have "balloon" payments because the bank or lending institution wants to entice the borrower with smaller monthly payments in the beginning. It is only after some time that the bank expects the borrower to pay the exorbitant "balloon" payments in the future. Since the borrower is usually in the home by the time the first "balloon" payment comes due, the borrower will be forced to pay the lump sum. If not, the bank repossesses the home. The borrower can always refinance the home with another bank, but that would be additional time and money. I suspect the borrower will just re-negotiate with the original bank for a conventional loan. At this point, the bank stands to gain additional fees with the new fixed-rate mortgage.

I do not recommend an "interest-only" loan or any loan that has "balloon" payments. Let's face it. If you can't afford the monthly payment, you probably should not be in the home anyway. True, everyone wants to have their "dream" home, but not everyone can afford their "dream" home in real life. The point of any mortgage is to own the property at the end of the mortgage. If the "interest-only" loan is your only option, why bother to get the loan at all? You are probably better off renting an apartment. When you rent an apartment, you can always pack up and lease from someone else. When you take out an 'interest-only" loan, you are legally obligated to make the payments.

Besides, there is no guarantee you can re-finance a home before the "balloon" payment is due. Let's face it. The economy can turn sour and banks may cease lending right when you need a loan. What if you lose your job? What if you don't save enough for the "balloon" payment? Any number of circumstances may come together to prevent you from making the "balloon" payment. Sure, you can probably get a better home with this type of a loan. On the other hand, do you want to spend sleepless nights worrying how to make those "balloon" payments? Save yourself the aggravation. Walk away from any loan that has a "balloon" payment. Walk away from any loan that prevents you from eventually owning the property.

What if I don't have the down payment? There are ways to find that 10% down payment. Is it risky? Yes. Is it worth it? Real estate is always worth the price if you plan to stay in that same location for an extended period of time.

Regrettably, all humans need a place to occupy. We can always choose to occupy someone else's land and pay dearly for the privilege of being there. On the other hand, we can choose to occupy our own parcel of land. We just need to be willing to pay the bank for the privilege of eventually owning the land free and clear. It is a worthwhile endeavor. The goal here is to eventually own a place to call your own when retirement rolls around.

I Bought My House with Credit Cards

PREQUALIFYING

Why do we need the government or the bank? Let's be honest. Real estate is expensive. Most people do not have enough money to buy real estate for cash. Thus, most people take out a home loan (oftentimes called a mortgage) from a bank or lending institution.

Before I even start looking for a mortgage, is it necessary to get prequalified?

No, it is not necessary to get prequalified, but there are certain advantages to being prequalified. First, you demonstrate your sincerity to the loan officer. It proves to the bank or lending institution that you are serious about getting the loan. You are no longer asking their competition to meet or exceed the terms and conditions of the loan.

The prequalification process allows the loan officer to assess your ability to get a loan *prior to verifying your information.* The loan officer will not make any phone calls to your employer at this time, but the loan officer may pull your credit report. In the preapproval process, the loan officer will call your employer and anyone else he or she deems necessary to get an accurate assessment of your ability to repay the loan. The prequalification process may not require any fees. The preapproval process *does* include a fee. This fee is non-refundable, so make sure you want to do business with this particular bank or credit union.

Before you even get prequalified, get information about the lender. This is the time to find the appropriate lender for your real estate deal.

What if the bank or credit union says I do qualify for a loan? Ask the bank or credit union what is the maximum loan amount. They will certainly tell you how much house you can get. When you pre-qualify for a loan, the bank or credit union will give you a letter to show the seller. There should be a maximum loan amount on that letter.

After that, go find real estate that fits the dollar amount and description on the letter. If you qualify for a home loan, find a home that fits the dollar amount shown on the letter. If it is not for a home loan, it may take more time to find a parcel of land for a certain dollar amount. You may need to go online to find a real estate agent for that type of land. Be sure that this real estate agent is licensed. *All licensed real estate agents have a card with their license number.* Be sure to write down this license number just in case the agent fails to represent you. Whatever you do, avoid all high pressure salesmen. Usually these people have slick advertising selling everything from lakefront lots to beachfront property. Check with the Better Business Bureau™ first. There are lots of shady operators that sell so-called "investments" to unsuspecting consumers. If the licensed real estate agent does anything criminal, you can complain to the state real estate commission. You can be sure that the licensed real estate agent may no longer be licensed for long.

Be forewarned. Never offer a measly 3% down payment for any real estate purchase. Most real estate purchases require a 5% to 10% down payment. Offering a low down payment is a red flag for any loan officer. No doubt, the loan officer will ask more probing questions. If you can only afford a 3% down payment (even with all the strategies outlined in this book), consider finding a less expensive parcel of land. Make sure the down payment is 5% or 10% of the asking price. You can always upgrade to a more expensive parcel of land later.

Please note that some areas in the country may have more buyers than sellers. This means you will have competition for a dwindling number of properties. Be sure to tell the seller that you already qualify for a loan. By showing the seller your prequalifying letter, you might be able to stop a bidding war. If the other people bidding for that property do not have a prequalifying letter, there is a good chance the seller will opt for your offer. Let's face it. There is no guarantee if the other party can even get a loan. The other party may promise a higher price, but a seller may opt for a prequalified buyer. The seller may have a tight timetable. The seller might not have time to the wait for the other party to get a loan.

Remember, the seller's real estate agent has a responsibility to show the seller all offers. Don't be afraid to send copies of that prequalifying letter to the seller. Oftentimes, you may never see the seller until closing. By all means, offer the seller's agent an opportunity to present a copy of your prequalifying letter to the seller. Certainly, the seller has every right to pick any of the offers. If the other party offers more for the seller's property, the seller has every right to ask if the other party has the ability to pay the higher price. If not, your prequalifying letter may just seal the deal.

If prequalification puts you ahead of other buyers, preapproval allows you to be ready for the loan. In the prequalification process, the lender has yet to authenticate your information. This includes calling your employer and getting a credit report from all three of the credit reporting agencies. This is also the time when the bank or lending institution will ask for a fee. Don't panic. Before asking for preapproval, get their preapproval fees upfront. This is not the time to balk at their fees. This is also not the time to make any additional credit card purchases, because this will show up on your credit report. Yes, it takes time for all of your recent credit purchases to reach the credit reporting agencies. If you really don't have the pre-approval fees, I recommend borrowing the pre-approval fees from friends or family. If necessary, agree to purchase whatever they want with your credit card only after the loan process is finished. This is a critical time, so hold off on any large purchases. This includes anything more expensive than a trip to the gas station. The bank or lending institution will expect that you do make a few essential credit card purchases, but big-ticket items like mattresses, automobiles, furniture, and boats should be avoided at all costs.

In fact, the loan officer will see how times people request your credit report. Typically, competing credit card companies will ask for your credit report without your consent. The loan officer may ignore these because the credit card companies do this constantly to get new customers. However, loan officers may get nervous when credit cards from retailers ask for your credit report. This usually means you entered a retail establishment with the intention of buying a big-ticket item.

I Bought My House with Credit Cards

In truth, you may have decided to turn down whatever was being sold. Still, the loan officer will see this and wonder. Don't be too surprised if the loan officer starts to question everything else. When this happens, the loan officer may dig up other items you may never have expected.

I once drove into a car dealer's lot. Before I could protest, a car salesman appeared out of thin air. I was just trying to turn my car around. In less than the time it takes to get a hamburger at a fast-food joint, I was out of my car and looking at a brand-new sports car. That was after my divorce and my credit report was not worth the printed paper. Still, the car dealer was able to pull up my credit report after receiving only my name. Of course, not all retailers are this fast. I am not trying to tell you to avoid all retailers during this time period. Just avoid the retailers that sell big-ticket items. If your friend asks you for a ride to the car dealer, politely turn them down. If you have to go, give the car dealer a false name.

DEALING WITH THE BANK

Can I avoid paperwork altogether? No. Today, you must do paperwork if you want to get a loan to purchase real estate. If you must do paperwork, you might as well start the prequalification and pre-approval process right away. Look at the preceding chapters for a list of what the bank or lending institution will expect from you.

Before the Great Recession of 2007-2009, some lending institutions did "no-doc" loans. "No-doc" loans did not have any documentation requirements. Many lending institutions based their decision to lend money to a borrower based solely on their credit score. This turned out to be a grave mistake. These lending institutions only saw one aspect of their potential customer. Sure, these borrowers may have had great credit scores, but they also had other financial obligations and mountains of debt that no one knew about. In truth, not all companies send their information to the credit reporting agencies. Some gas card transactions and car loans are never reported to any of the credit reporting agencies. To no one's surprise, these lending institutions closed their doors or were bought by larger lending institutions. More people defaulted on their "no-doc" loans than from any other type of loans.

Do you really want that house? A bank can determine how serious you are about paying them back by the amount of the down payment. In fact, the bank or lending institution may ignore certain credit blemishes if you present a 33% down payment. Indeed, much of mortgage payment at the beginning of the loan period does not go toward paying down the principal. This is pure profit for the bank. If you pay a 20% down payment, the bank or lending institution will get their profit much faster. *The bank or lender institution should waive any PMI* (private mortgage insurance) if you present a 20% down payment. If they don't waive the PMI, move onto the next lender.

If you want to purchase a home, ask the lender about annual percentage rate (APR) interest rates on their home loans. Be sure to ask their lowest and highest rates. Why would you ask for their highest rate? If you are reading this book, there is a good chance you might be stuck with their highest interest rates.

Be sure to ask if this APR includes all of the added fees. Why does this matter? Banks and lending institutions are notorious for not advertising the final annual percentage rate. For example, banks and lending institutions may charge additional points. What is a point? A point is simply a percent of the real estate price. Why would banks and lending institutions add a percentage to the total cost? Banks and lending institutions may charge a point for originating the loan. This means they charge extra for starting the loan process. This usually means the bank or lending institution will send your loan to be serviced by another bank or lending institution. The banks and lending institutions may charge a point to even do the necessary paperwork.

Why all the extra charges? This insures that the bank or lending institution is reimbursed for their time before you even shell out your first mortgage payment. These charges should include the appraisal for the property. The bank or lending institution will pull your credit report and they will push this cost onto you. The bank or lending institution may require another survey to check the boundaries of your parcel of land. You might want a pest inspection (a necessity even in Alaska).

Processing fees are added to offset the costs of the notary, the underwriter, the real estate broker, the real estate attorney, and the banker (for wire transfers). The underwriter will include the costs of processing your mortgage insurance application. The broker will want money to do a title search. This means the broker will check though the county records to make sure you can even receive a free and clear title once the mortgage is paid in full. Still, the broker will want money to get you title insurance (in case the broker missed something and someone challenges your claim to the property).

Don't be too surprised if bank or lending institution will not disclose their appraisal fees, title search fees, insurance fees, notary fees, recording fees, etc. Even though the Truth in Lending Act provides some protections for consumers, banks and lending institutions can legally block the disclosure of some of these fees. Since they may use third-party attorneys and brokers, banks and lending institution may not even know the true costs for these items. Still, they will pass along these costs to you as the consumer. *The Truth in Lending Statement should outline the estimates for these costs. The bank or lending institution should update you on any changes to that Truth in Lending Statement.*

Depending on the date of closing, you might need to pay interest, property taxes, mortgage insurance, and even flood insurance. Since all of this depends on the date of closing, the bank or lending institution might not have these costs, yet.

Don't forget the taxes and fees associated with real estate transactions in general. Yes, the local municipality will want money in the form of city and/or county tax stamps. Yes, the local municipality will want money just to complete the transaction with a "transfer" tax.

Additional points *could* be beneficial to you as the consumer. You may be asked to pay a discount point to lower the interest rate on your mortgage. Be sure to ask if this is even possible. This might be worthwhile. As always, redo your monthly mortgage payment calculation. A lower interest rate can make the difference between making the monthly mortgage payment with cash left over to pay off the cash advance or not.

The bank or lending institution may ask you to "lock in" the interest rate. Since the interest rate for home loans fluctuate, many people try to catch the lowest rate by paying extra. At this time, you must see if you can borrow the extra money needed. Double-check if your cash advance limit can cover all of these closing costs. I recommend using the bank or lending institution's higher interest rate to calculate your monthly payment. Make sure the monthly payment is less than 38% of your take-home pay. If you are reading this book, there is no guarantee the bank or lending institution will even give you the lower interest rate anyway.

Next, ask the bank or lending institution about closing costs. At a certain point, the bank or lending institution will give you a "good-faith" estimate. The cost to complete or "close" the deal should be spelled out in detail on this estimate. Closing costs can include the price of sending and filing the paperwork with the local courthouse or magistrate's office. *If the paperwork is never filed with the local municipality, you will never receive the deed to the property.* Filing is the only way to make this real estate transaction legal and binding, so expect the bank or lending institution to charge this back to you. Count up all the closing costs and compare that this number to your cash advance limit. If the costs at closing exceed your cash advance limit, move onto the next bank or lending institution.

After that, check if there is a prepayment penalty for this loan. Even though you may have no intention of paying this loan off early, you might change your mind in the future. Don't forget to ask how long the prepayment penalty is in effect and for what amount. The prepayment penalty could be a percent of mortgage or a set price based on a certain number of mortgage payments. Banks and lending institutions stand to reap higher profits if they can keep you as a customer for a longer period of time. To keep you, the bank or lending institution may offer a lesser interest rate so you will keep their prepayment penalties. It never hurts to ask.

Don't bother asking for their minimum down payment. Count on making a 10% down payment. Add this to the closing costs and compare the sum to your cash advance limit. If the down payment and closing costs exceed your cash advance limit, move onto the next bank or lending institution. If you cannot find a bank or lending institution that can work with you, try finding a less expensive parcel of land.

Finally, ask the bank or lending institution how long it will take them to process the loan. This is very important. This will determine if you will be successful or not. Do not skip this step! Stop and find a different bank or lending institution **if it will take more than thirty days**. Your cash advance will be conveyed to all the credit reporting agencies in less than thirty days. If your bank or lending institution discovers that you have borrowed the down payment, they will not allow you to continue the loan process. Find a different bank or lending institution.

Sorry, the real estate business will never go entirely paperless. Since the beginning, humans have fought and died for land. To make it known to everyone, humans have tried to make their land claims permanent. First, they painted on cave walls. Next, they carved their names in stone. Soon, humans made giant monuments to commemorate their victories. They built giant obelisks and pyramids as a testament to their triumphs. As long as there are humans, there will some written form of communication for people to lay claim to their parcel of land. Unfortunately, this extends into the loan approval process.

DOWN PAYMENTS & CASH ADVANCES

Okay, so you're determined to buy real estate. From an earlier discussion, I talked about down payments. Besides your bad credit (or lack of credit), this could be the biggest obstacle to obtaining a loan for a parcel of land. You have looked in your bank account and determined that you could not pay the minimum 10% required for a down payment.

This is where the cash advance comes in handy. No doubt you have seen the many places around town that advertise "cash advances" or "payday loans" businesses. These businesses specialize in lending money on a weekly or even daily basis. What do they do? These businesses take something as collateral like a car title or something valuable. Pawn shops may lend you money on gold coins, firearms, collectibles, or jewelry. When you fail to repay the money, the pawn shop sells the items used for collateral. Consumer loan businesses will do the same thing with your car title, too.

For you, the cash advance that we will use originates from your credit card. In short, the credit card company is betting against your credit score. If you fail to pay the interest and the balance you owe, the credit card company will take away your good credit score. No doubt, the credit card company will report these delinquent obligations to all three credit reporting agencies.

Be warned. The cash advance has a significantly larger interest rate. The interest rate is at least 1% (sometimes up to 10%) over the regular interest rate for normal purchases. Even worse, the cash advance accrues interest from the day it is borrowed. There is never any grace period like normal credit card purchases. Most credit cards allow you to pay off the balance each month. The cash advance is different, so don't use it unless you know you can pay it off immediately. This effectively makes the cash advance 50% more expensive.

From personal experience, I do not advise waiting more than a month before paying off a cash advance. I once borrowed $1000 against my credit card account for a down payment on a condominium I wanted to buy. In less than one month, the interest alone was $330. That's the significance of the interest charges that credit card companies can levy on a cash advance.

If that was not bad enough, you will probably be hit with a cash advance fee. Usually this is greater than 3% and/or a minimum $10 fee. As with all financial transactions, read the fine print. If you have questions, call the credit card company. If you are polite, they will be more than happy to outline all the fees (hidden or otherwise). Make the calculations or just ask the credit card company directly. Sometimes, it may not be worth it to take a cash advance of $100 or $200 because of the fee structure. Getting charged 23% or more on your cash advance is normal.

Every so often, a credit card company may advertise 0% cash advance fees for one year. This means the cash advance has the same interest rate as normal purchases. As with everything else, read the fine print because there are certainly exclusions and requirements. More often than not, these offers are only available to those with stellar credit. These credit card companies are betting that you cannot pay off the cash advance in less than a year. Historically, customers who use cash advances are the same customers who have large balances. Usually, the credit card company reels in the new customer with the introductory 0% cash advance fee. The subsequent fees after one year will more than make up for the credit card company's loss in revenue for the first year. Besides, *all your payments to the credit card company go to the balance with the lower interest rate. The balance with the higher interest rate continues to accrue.* For this reason, **use the credit card with no or low balance to get the cash advance** . This will allow you to pay off the cash advance faster.

Remember, you should only do one cash advance from a single credit card company at any one time. Be sure to get all of the costs of the down payment and closing costs up front. Getting more than one cash advance from different credit card companies will raise suspicions at the bank.

That being said, there are ways to find the best deals on the internet. Be sure to investigate if the credit card has any special offers on balance transfers. There could be a 0% introductory interest rate on balance transfer. If your current credit card has a lower cash advance interest rate, you can always transfer your old balance to the new credit card with the 0% introductory interest rate.

Of course, check on the internet for no or low annual fees. If the new credit card has a 0% introductory interest rate on the balance transfer, it might also have a low introductory rate on the outstanding balance. Check how long the low rates will be in effect. It may not be advertised on the internet, but it might be worth a phone call. Most credit card companies have toll free numbers for people wanting to apply to their cards (but most credit card companies do not have toll free numbers for complaints or transaction disputes). Remember, the salesperson at the credit card company may check your credit report over the phone. Unfortunately, loan officers may see how many times your credit report has been accessed. I suggest looking for an alternative credit card well in advance of asking for a mortgage. Loan officers start to worry if there are too many requests for your credit history from credit card companies. Even if you apply for a credit card online, the credit card company will automatically check your credit report. Please do your shopping for a credit card well ahead of any real estate purchase.

If cash advances are so expensive, why would anyone use a cash advance? I suspect that the cash advance was originally designed to help travelers in foreign countries. Sometimes, you need the local currency to trade when you are overseas. Unless you can trade your dollars for the local currency at the nearest bank, you probably won't be able to trade with merchants that don't use dollars. Over time, people started using the cash advance even when they were not traveling overseas. After people started abusing this convenience, the credit card companies curbed the abuse of the cash advance by levying hefty fees.

I Bought My House with Credit Cards

In some rare instances, a cash advance may make sense. For example, some transactions will not take place with credit cards. Non-business people don't normally have ways to accept credit cards. Self-employed auto mechanics, tow truck owners, taxi cab operators, and the neighborhood barber may not take credit cards. These merchants may not want to pay the extra fees. For them, all transactions are cash or personal check.

Cash advances may be necessary if you have members of your immediate family that do not have credit cards. Perhaps they are too young. Maybe they are trying to pay off their credit cards. A cash advance on your credit card may allow the transaction to take place. Of course, you hope you will be paid back in a reasonable amount of time to offset the added cost. In most cases, a cash advance on your credit card should only be used if no other option is available.

I cannot stress enough the need to read the fine print. If a credit card does offer a cash advance, check the annual percentage rate. It may not be readily available on your monthly statement. In fact, it may be hidden in the paperwork that they are required to send to you. There is an obvious reason why credit card companies print the paperwork in small print and often on thin paper. The useful life of the thin paper makes storing the paperwork problematic. The thin paper rips easily and will deteriorate faster. Most people end up throwing this paperwork out. By all means, keep all the paperwork. Use a magnifying lens to see what hidden fees are associated with the cash advance process. During the loan process, you do not want any surprises. Look for a telephone number. Call if you have questions. The paperwork associated with your credit card may be written by a lawyer. Since most people are not lawyers, the fine print may be unintelligible to anyone but a lawyer.

If cash advances are so expensive, why are they still available? Since the Great Recession of 2007-2009, the use of these cash advances may have dropped off almost by a third in the years following the recession. Most people are very sensitive to the constant drain brought on by credit card debt. Even people who have good credit are shying away from larger and larger credit card balances. This may worry many in the credit card industry, but the mountain of debt still makes the credit card business very lucrative. Since interest accrues each billing cycle, the original purchase amounts balloon to hefty sums if they are not paid off right away. Since credit card companies only require a "minimum payment", most people who use credit cards will never pay off their balances. In the meantime, the credit card companies are happy to pull out more interest payments from their unwary consumers.

In the recent years, there has been a trend towards informing the consumer about these credit cards. In fact, credit card issuers are required by law to publish the payoff date if only the "minimum payment" is paid each month. This forces credit card issuers to actually have "minimum payments" that allow the current debt to be paid off in the near future. Before the Great Recession of 2007-2009, the "minimum payment" was considered a joke by most people. The "minimum payment" was once an arbitrary amount based solely on the consumer's payment record. Today, a consumer will actually see when they can finally get out of debt (as long as they do not make any other purchases).

When calculating what you need to pay for a cash advance, find the annual percentage rate from the paperwork that they are required to send to you. Be sure to calculate interest that accumulates from the day you pull out the cash advance. In other words, find the total interest payment you will pay on the amount. Instead of dividing by twelve due of the number of months in the year, divide by the 365 due of the number days in the year. Take the number of days since you pulled out the money and multiply by the interest payment per day.

If you can't find a percentage rate for cash advances, just assume that you will pay 50% more than you would for a normal purchase. Some industry analysts have calculated that the "effective" interest rate may exceed 40%.

If all else fails, pick up the phone and call the credit card company. Ask how much it would cost you to get a cash advance for a certain number of days. I am sure that they will be more than happy to calculate just how much you will pay for that privilege. I recommend sitting down when you receive this information. You might not like what you hear.

Since the Great Recession of 2007-2009, new legislation has made cash advances less profitable for credit card companies. This legislation was designed to protect the consumer. Still, people who use the cash advance are considered "high-risk" customers. If you regularly put your credit card in the ATM machine, you might need to put this book on the shelf until you get better money-management skills. Remember, the number of times you put your credit card into the machine is counted and shown on your credit report. Getting a cash advance while on vacation in a foreign country may not raise any eyebrows. On the other hand, getting a cash advance more than once a month may alert your credit card company. If you normally get a cash advance for groceries or frivolous items, you might need to get credit counseling first. If there is no guilt associated with borrowing someone else's money, the methods in this book are not for you.

Instead, the long-term goal of this book is to get you to purchase assets that appreciate in value. Before you get the interest rate to your cash advance, you need to get serious about your spending habits. Once you get a mortgage on a piece of land, you will be tied to that piece of land for the next thirty years. Even if you default on the loan, your credit will be damaged for at least seven years. If you get any credit cards *after* bankruptcy, there won't be any protection from the issuing credit card company. The credit card company can sue you for everything you have and possibly garnish your wages until the balance is paid in full. If you doubt me, read the fine print. The fine print will spell out your rights (or lack of rights) if you take out a line of credit after bankruptcy.

Now that you have received the interest rate for your cash advance, go and find yourself a suitable parcel of land. I recommend searching on the internet first. Look on builder's websites. Look at their websites and see their promotions. Look for builder financing and low down-payments.

CASH ADVANCES

How much of a cash advance should get? First of all, check the fine print to see what can be borrowed against your credit card. Fortunately, the credit card company will usually print this amount in a conspicuous place. The credit card companies really do want you to keep to this amount and no more. This amount is calculated based on your spending habits and ability to pay them back. Believe it or not, the credit card companies keep track of all of your spending and monitor your credit score like a hawk. If you make purchases in a foreign country or somewhere you don't usually go, don't be too surprised if the credit card company gives you call to see if you really are at that location. Don't be too surprised if the cash advance limit is much less than your credit limit. The cash advance limit is there to protect the credit card company. Through trial and error, credit card companies have discovered that people who use cash advances are more likely to default on their obligations.

If the cash advance limit is less than the down payment required, you might need to move on to the next credit card. Most consumers have more than one credit card. Perhaps you have a credit card that you don't normally use. As always, keeping accurate records is crucial.

I do not recommend taking a cash advance from more than one credit card. Certainly, it is possible to do this, but I do not recommend depositing more than one credit card check at the bank. One credit card check will raise eyebrows. Two credit card checks from different credit companies will certainly invite unwanted attention. The bank may even make you wait even longer to clear your checks. The bank may even ask for additional identification. If this happens, comply with their demands and be polite. *You are not doing anything criminal* . You are just borrowing the down payment.

Before the Great Recession of 2007-2009, it was possible to get a mortgage with a minimum down payment of 3% of the asking price. Usually, the mortgage with the low down payment is an Adjustable Rate Mortgage (ARM). The lending institution is probably betting that the prime interest rate will more than likely go up in the future and they will recoup their money. Why? Adjustable rate mortgages are based on the prime interest rate or some other published index. Why would a lending institution use an adjustable rate mortgage? A low initial interest rate will usually attract a lot of customers. Sure, there is no guarantee that the interest rate will stay that low. Still, the lending institution has grabbed you as a customer from other lending institutions that only offer mortgages with higher fixed rates.

Should I go with an adjustable rate mortgage? I did, because I knew I wanted to refinance the loan within three years. Doing the math, a $200,000 adjustable rate mortgage at a low introductory rate and minimum down payment of 3% would require only a $600 down payment. Of course, there are closing costs and the price of a home inspection. If you are using a builder to construct a new house, you won't need the costs of a home inspection. You probably need to do a walk-through with the builder prior to closing instead.

Now that you have found how much extra money you need, it is time to get the extra money in the form of a cash advance. For this, there are three different ways to get a cash advance.

The first way is to visit your local automatic teller machine (ATM). Before you make a trip to the ATM, make sure the ATM is tied to your financial network. There is nothing worse than trying to access an automatic teller machine and finding out the machine has no access to your financial institution. Before you even take the time to drive out there, check your statement for the financial network of your credit card company. Next, find your personal identification number (PIN). Usually this is issued in advance. This is where good record-keeping becomes invaluable. Oftentimes, the PIN is included in a separate mailing. More often than not, the PIN will be printed on paper that is sandwiched inside a security envelope. The security envelope may have carbon paper inside that allows the PIN to be imprinted inside without any employees ever seeing the exact number.

If you cannot locate your PIN, call your credit card company and ask that the PIN be reset. They may mail you a new PIN if they cannot verify your identity over the phone. Usually, they ask you for your billing address or other information (such as your mother's maiden name) to verify your identity.

When you receive your PIN, head over to the designated ATM. Follow the credit card company's instructions on withdrawing your cash. Oftentimes, a separate mailer will arrive showing specific instructions to proceed with the cash advance. If you did not receive these instructions, call the credit card company if you have any other questions. Select "Credit" when the ATM gives you a choice between checking, savings, and credit.

Remember, you will be charged additional fees for this transaction, so withdraw the maximum if this is required for your real estate purchase. As always, make sure no one peeks over your shoulder to see your PIN. Don't hold out your credit card until you step in front of the ATM. Thieves can remember which buttons you press. Once they see your PIN, it is just matter of time before they will move in and try to steal your card. Once your card is stolen, there is no stopping the thief from withdrawing more cash. If you are in a rough neighborhood, it may be best to find another ATM location. There is no need to be the victim of a crime.

Be forewarned that the mortgage company or lending institution may not accept cash at the closing. Check if they need a certified check. Make sure the lending institution with your checking account is not the same lending institution that will be involved with closing on your new real estate purchase. If they are the same, the lending institution will immediately see that you really did not have the down payment in the first place. They will not look too kindly on you borrowing the down payment from your credit card issuer.

I Bought My House with Credit Cards

The second method of getting a cash advance is to do the transaction over the phone with your credit card company. Before you pick up the phone, be sure you know your checking account number and your bank's routing number. The routing number is a unique identifying number for the bank. There is usually a large series of numbers at the bottom of the check next to the signature line. The large number consists of at least two parts. The last part will be your checking account number and the first part will be the routing number. Have all this information ready when you make the call. Follow the credit card company's instructions and they will deposit the cash advance directly into your checking account in two to three business days. Remember to ask for the additional fees involved with this transaction. Your credit card company will not readily volunteer this information so don't forget to ask. You will need to know all of these fees so your credit card statement will not present you with unexpected surprises.

Oftentimes, you can go directly to a bank which does business with your credit card company. If you have questions, your credit card company can tell you which bank will do the transaction and specific instructions on how to do the transaction. Be sure to bring photo identification, because the bank that the credit card company chooses may not be the one that has your checking account.

The final method is probably the easiest method. Oftentimes, credit card companies will mail credit card checks to you which you can use. My wife calls these "funny money" checks. They look like normal checks, but they are linked directly to your credit card account. Yes, these are very dangerous, because they arrive in the mail. Criminals can steal these checks and use them quite readily. Personally, I recommend people shred these credit card checks if they never plan to use them. If you do plan to use them in the future, I recommend that you store these in a safe and away from anyone who may be tempted to use them.

Before using any of these credit card checks, look for any expiration date. On occasion, these credit card checks are tied to promotional rates that last only for a certain time. Every so often, these credit card checks may be tied to certain types of merchandise, especially if the credit card is not the normal VISA™ or MasterCard™ variety. Look for anything else that may limit the purchase amount or location.

Next, take the credit card check and deposit this into your checking account. When I did this, the bank teller immediately informed me that there would be hold on my check. The bank wanted a few business days to verify the validity of the check and if such a large amount could be drawn against my credit card account. Luckily, I was ready to sign the loan papers. All I had to do was bring a certified check to the closing.

Please note that you need to remain cool and calm. The bank will ask for photo identification. Naturally, the people at the bank will be very suspicious. This is normal. Check fraud is a serious crime. The people at the bank are only doing their job. Do not be rude or insist on fast action. You are not doing anything illegal. The bank personnel are just being cautious. Ask politely the date when your credit card check from the credit card company will clear. If needed, get a phone number of someone you can call to see if the credit card check did clear. If this is not possible, you can also go to the ATM to see if the money was deposited into the checking account.

After the check clears, go to the bank one last time and request a certified check for the amount you need at closing. Don't delay. Remember that the clock is ticking from the moment you withdraw the down payment from your credit card account. Unlike a regular credit card purchase, a cash advance accrues interest daily and there is no grace period.

The loophole here is that it takes approximately thirty days for the three credit reporting agencies to find out about your added debt to your credit card balances. Of course, none of these lending institutions want you to accrue any additional debt from the time that they check your credit report. Lending institutions make decisions on your ability to pay them back based on your current financial obligations. If they find out you borrowed the down payment, the lending institution will immediately stop the loan process. You will not get the loan and the real estate will be sold to someone else.

There is a good chance that the lending institution will make you sign an affidavit stating that you will not accrue any additional financial obligations between the time that they check your credit report and the date of the closing. This is to protect the lending institution. In case you default on the loan, the government will protect the lending institution from losing their principal. The lending institution wants to be absolved of any fraud perpetrated by you, the consumer. Remember, you are not participating in any criminal activity. Yes, you are borrowing the down payment. Yes, signing this affidavit would certainly be the wrong thing to do. When I received this affidavit, the closing agent was in such a rush. Luckily, they did not see me scribble something on the signature line. I could literally see the dollar signs in their eyes. I was just one of the many people who were buying a house from them. I was sure there were more people in the next room waiting for their turn to sign the paperwork to their own house.

Take the keys to the new house. *Remember that the clock is ticking on the cash advance. You need to pay off the cash advance because the interest payments accrue daily.*

CAN I AVOID THE CASH ADVANCE FEES?

Are there alternatives? Yes, using a cash advance to borrow the down payment is expensive. Yes, there are other ways to do this.

As we said before, there are credit card checks that have promotional or one-time-only interest rates that are reasonable. These interest rates are comparable to interest rates for normal credit card purchases. Check carefully through your paperwork from the credit card company. Unfortunately, these offers have expiration dates. The expiration dates should be on the credit card check, too. If these credit card checks are expired, it would not hurt to call the credit card company to see when they will be running the promotional rate again. If your balance is paid in full, the credit card company may even send you a credit card check with the promotional rate to entice you to use their card again. Let's face it. Credit card companies don't make any money if they cannot charge interest on your balance.

The first alternative is to circumvent the cash advance fees altogether. You can use your credit card to purchase regular merchandise and receive the cash equivalent from your friends.

How does this work?

Here is an example. Let's say your friend wants to buy $1000 in gold coins from a dealer. The dealer does not accept personal checks, but the dealer does accept credit cards. At the same time, you need $1000 to complete your real estate purchase. You have discovered that the cash advance fees would be roughly $300. Of course, you don't want to pay those exorbitant cash advance fees and your friend really wants to buy those gold coins. Your friend feels queasy carrying around that much cash in his pocket. As the good friend that you are, you drive your friend to your bank to deposit his personal check into your bank account. Next, you drive your friend to the dealer and pay for the gold coins with your credit card. Your friend goes home with his gold coins without carrying a mountain of cash. You wait for your friend's check to clear. After the check clears, you get a certified check from your bank to take to the closing. At closing, you present the certified check to the closing agent. The transaction is completed and you move into your new house. In the following months, you pay off your credit card without all of the high cash advance fees.

Here is another example. Your parents want to buy new appliances worth $1100. They can write a check for the new appliances, but your father thinks the new appliances are only worth $1000. You need $1000 to complete your real estate transaction. You find out that the fees will be $300 for a $1000 cash advance. As a gesture of good will, you humbly volunteer to give your parents a $100 discount on the appliances. You pull out your rarely used credit card from your local hardware store. You use the credit card to buy the appliances and have them delivered to your parent's house. At the same time, you take your parent's check for $1000 to the bank. After the check clears, you get a certified check for $1000 for closing. You hand the certified check to the closing agent and receive the keys to your new house. Immediately, you start paying down your credit card from the hardware store. You saved $100 in cash advance fees. Your parents saved $100 on their new appliances.

Here is another example. You have an old Pontiac Firebird. You need new parts to get it running again. You also need $2000 to complete your real estate transaction. Your brother's friend wants to buy the Firebird from you, but only if it is running. Your brother's friend can fix the Firebird himself, but he needs money for the parts. Curious, you talk to your brother's friend and have him check out the car. You agree to buy the parts from the local auto parts store if he agrees to pay $2000 for the car title. At the bank, you accept the $2000 check from your brother's friend and deposit the check in your account. Afterwards, you drive to the auto parts store with your brother's friend. With your credit card, your brother's friend gets the all parts he needs to fix the old Firebird. Your brother's friend has all the parts sent to his house. At the same time, you have your brother tow the old Pontiac Firebird to his friend's house. Then, you drop off your brother's friend with the car title in his hand. Finally, you go to the bank when the check clears and request a certified check for the closing. Your brother's friend owns the Pontiac Firebird and you own a new rental property.

In all of these examples, you calculated the cash advance fees ahead of time. You also had friends or family members you can trust. There is nothing worse than taking a check to the bank that does not clear. I do not recommend doing this with anyone you do not trust. Look for opportunities to use your credit cards to purchase items for people who already have the cash in their bank accounts. You might need to offer your friends and family a "discount" on their purchases. This will entice them to work with you in avoiding the nasty cash advance fees you are trying to avoid.

Another alternative is to use an internet pay service. There are internet pay services that send money anywhere. Can they send money to a checking account? These internet pay services send money around the world. There's no reason they cannot send money to someone you know. Of course, there are may be limits to how much they can send. For example, Amazon Payments™ (which competes with PayPal™) can only send a limit of $500 without any additional charges. If they send $500 from your credit card to your friend's checking account, you can have your friend go to the bank and give you the cash. The transaction will appear on your credit card statement as a regular purchase. This will effectively bypass the exorbitant fees associated with a cash advance.

That being said, the credit card companies may have rules against avoiding the cash advance fees that they charge. As always, read the fine print. The credit card companies may take legal action against you. Also, you need to completely trust whoever will receive the money. There is nothing worse than sending the money and not getting the cash. I recommend a family member or spouse.

In addition, these internet pay services can be here today and gone tomorrow. Their policies and prices may change without notice. I recommend asking your friends to see which internet pay services they use. Get information on their rates and fees. Ask how happy they are with the service. So far, these internet payment services are inadequately advertised.

I suspect that these internet pay services are not in the public eye for a reason. Municipalities are scrambling for revenue due to their over-spending. Since the internet enters their communities, municipalities immediately think they have the right to tax any business transaction in their community. Whether or not this is legal remains to be seen. I suspect this will be playing out more and more in courtrooms all across the world.

I also suspect that these internet pay services allow the porn industry to get their revenue. With millions of dollars flowing into burgeoning coffers, these internet pay services have a vested interest to keep these transactions private. As long as these services remain in the shadows, no one will grab their profits.

Another alternative is to borrow the money from your individual retirement account (IRA). Be forewarned that you can only borrow money against a retirement account for sixty days. Like cash advances, be sure you have the ability to pay the money back quickly.

I strongly recommend not "cashing out" any retirement accounts. When I did this, I was hit with a 10% penalty for early withdrawal. The bank promptly subtracted this from the amount I received. If that was not bad enough, the additional cash pushed me into another tax bracket. I paid additional 10% in taxes at the end of the year. Needless to say, I had no tax refund that year.

I Bought My House with Credit Cards

WHAT DO I TELL THE LOAN OFFICER?

If you are trying to get a loan from the bank, the bank will probably have information on your checking and savings account. The loan officer will want to see if there is enough cash in these accounts to pay for the down payment and closing costs.

If you are reading this book, you probably don't have the cash for the down payment and closing costs. Don't panic. Just tell them you will get help with the down payment from your parents. If possible, call your parents and make them a deal. Promise to buy them whatever they want with your credit card. You just want the cash equivalent of the down payment and closing costs. Of course, you will pay for these purchases with a credit card after the loan officer checks your credit report. Please note that the clock is ticking once you make these credit card purchases, so try to delay the credit card purchases for as long as possible.

If your parents are deceased, tell them that you will get help with the down payment from your spouse. Please note that the loan officer will always try to include your spouse in the loan process. They will do this whether you want to or not. Why? By law, you and your spouse share financial responsibilities. Move on to the next suggestion if you do not want to include your spouse. If possible, don't mention your spouse at all. If you don't want to include your spouse, the loan officer will start asking more questions. In fact, the loan officer may pull a credit report on your spouse. Of course, the loan officer may or may not be able to do this under the laws of your state. In fact, you should know beforehand if the loan officer can do this. If the loan officer insists on getting your spouse involved, tell them you will ask for their consent first. Even at this stage, you may still have reservations about including your spouse.

From personal experience, my second wife negotiated with our credit union all by herself. She bought a house without me. What was her excuse for not including me? She simply told the credit union that I had a terrible credit history due to a nasty divorce. Immediately, the bank dropped their request to include me on the loan application. Sure, I contributed to the down payment, but the credit union did not want to pull my credit report. If I recall correctly, credit union policies stated that all credit reports have to be used. Since the credit union would be obligated to use my "terrible" credit report, the credit union specifically chose not to pull my credit report. The credit union was under the impression that my "terrible" credit report may impact the loan process in a negative way.

If you are not married, tell them you will get help from your boyfriend or girlfriend. By this time, the loan officer will request that the money be deposited in your checking account as soon as possible. Tell the loan officer you will try to accommodate that request as soon as possible. Of course, you might not have a boyfriend or girlfriend at all. Still, the loan officer has no way of verifying that information, so feel free to use this to your advantage.

At this point in the loan process, you will need to use the cash advance strategies I have outlined in the previous chapter in this book.

Be careful. Before you get started with the loan process, check where your spouse has their checking and savings account. In the same way, check where your girlfriend (or boyfriend) has their checking and savings account. If it is at a bank or credit union associated with the credit card you are going to use for the cash advance, you might need to go to a different ATM from another bank or credit union to withdraw the cash. Be sure to check how much cash you can withdraw beforehand. For example, there may be a three hundred dollar per day limit at the ATM. If you need more than three hundred dollars, you may need to withdraw cash more than once. You might be charged a fee each time, so be sure you know what the fees will be.

Deposit the cash advance into your checking account. Remember, the clock is ticking. You now have less than thirty days to close on the house.

If your spouse or girlfriend (or boyfriend) has their checking and savings account at a different bank, use a credit card check associated with the credit card account you want to use. Make sure this credit card account has a zero balance. You need a credit card account with a zero balance because all payments to the credit card will be applied to the non-cash advance balance first. In this way, the credit card company will reap the substantial fees they levy for the cash advance. You want to pay off this cash advance and the exorbitant fees right away. Pay as little as possible for the privilege of receiving a cash advance.

Put the amount you need for the down payment and closing costs on the check. I am assuming that you have received this amount from the loan officer and/or this amount was written on the "good faith estimate". Deposit this credit card check at your girlfriend's (or boyfriend's) bank. If you are married, deposit this credit card check at your wife's (or husband's) bank.

Wait until the check clears. This could take 3 business days. Find out from your loan officer who needs to receive the check. Usually, this is the bank or lending institution of the loan officer. If you are buying an existing home, the certified check may be written to the seller, but only if the seller owns the property outright and their mortgage is paid off.

Ask your girlfriend (or boyfriend) get you a certified check for the amount you deposited. If you are married, ask your wife (or husband) write you a certified check for the amount you deposited. Make sure the certified check is written out for the correct bank, lending institution, or seller.

Take the certified check to the real estate closing. You will use this certified check to pay for the down payment and closing costs.

If you cannot get a certified check, ask for a personal check from your girlfriend (or boyfriend). If you are married, ask for personal check from your wife (or husband), Take their personal check to your own bank or credit union and make the deposit.

Remember, the clock is ticking. You now have less than thirty days to close on the house.

Whatever you do, do not spend this money. While you are waiting for the closing date,   *I recommend limiting all of your spending to the bare minimum* . Remember, you will be responsible for additional expenses that may be associated with the real estate transaction. Local municipalities may impose additional fees that the bank or lending institution will not know about. If local municipalities fail to raise enough revenue from taxes, local municipalities will raise fees for their court costs and the amount required to record deeds.

Whatever you do, do not use any of your credit cards. Take note of the credit card which was responsible for your cash advance. Store this credit card in a fire-proof safe and don't use it. Check all of your credit card statements. Make a note of all the fees and all of your outstanding balances. *Your goal will be to wipe out the balance associated with the cash advance first* . The fees will probably amount to 33% of the cash advance, so don't be too surprised.

I recommend finding a second job during this time period and until your cash advance balance is paid in full. I know of people who worked evenings at a grocery store in the next county. I know of people who worked at the convenience store in the wee hours of the night. In both instances, none of their friends knew they were working a second job. By working a second job, they were not tempted to run up their credit cards. They did not eat at restaurants or catch the latest movies. They kept themselves busy and none of their friends noticed.

I Bought My House with Credit Cards

UNFORSEEN EXPENSES

Before you even start looking for real estate, please be warned.

Don't try this if you plan on moving in the near future. Renters don't have to put their homes for sale. Homeowners have the added expenses incurred by moving and finding another home in another location. These expenses can add up quickly. The expenses add up much quicker if you don't sell your old house first. First, check if your job will require you to move. If you don't travel for your job, this may not be a problem. Sitting at the same desk day after day may not be glamorous, but it allows you to pay off your house quicker than moving every other year.

Don't make the mistake of thinking that you can immediately rent out your house. The best types of rental homes are starter homes that are comparable in square footage to two-bedroom or three-bedroom apartments. Houses larger than twelve hundred square feet may be difficult to rent.

Take a realistic look at your budget. Don't ever factor in any raises in the near future. Since the Great Recession of 2007-2009, wages have yet to rebound to their nose bleed highs before the recession. If you earn minimum wage, there is no guarantee that the minimum wage will be raised. When calculating what you can actually afford, don't include bonus money or extra income from part-time work. Use your base salary and current take-home pay. Go to the internet and use one of the many free mortgage calculators. Type in the cost of the home you want to buy. Use the bank's advertised annual percentage rate. Don't use any of their introductory rates, because they will always go back up to their normally-advertised rate. Plug in the information and see what the mortgage payment will be. Add this mortgage payment to all the other financial obligations you have. Include all car payments, credit-card payments, and student loans. You don't have to count the rent payments unless of course you can't break your lease. If at all possible, time the closing date to when you need to renew the lease.

What number did you get?

If these expenses are less than half of your take-home pay, you will do well. Of course, you won't be going out to any fancy restaurants or seeing any fabulous shows. You will be taking your lunch to work in a paper bag. You may be working a second job to pay off the hefty cash advance you may need to acquire your new parcel of land.

If your expenses are more than half of your take-home pay, put this book on the shelf and wait. From here, you have three choices. The first choice involves increasing your take-home pay (more about that later). The second choice involves decreasing your monthly monetary obligations. Wait until that car payment is gone. Wait until those student loans are finished. Lower your credit card balances. The third and final choice is to find a different parcel of land. This will usually involve getting a more affordable house. You may need to look in a less expensive neighborhood. You might need to find a house with less square footage. Yes, there are dream-houses in every city, but those may need to wait. Besides, you can always trade up later.

Be sure you are prepared for the added costs of real estate. If you are currently renting, you can no longer call the landlord if something breaks. If you buy the home, you are your own landlord. As a landlord, you will have to pick up the phone if the toilets back up and spill over onto your floors. Most homeowner's policies will not cover weather-related damage. Worst of all, most homeowner's policies will not cover flooding of any kind, especially if it is caused by leaking pipes or bad plumbing.

As the new homeowner, all utility costs and property taxes are paid by you. If you don't want any surprises, ask the previous owner what these numbers would be. Most of the time, the previous owner would be happy to volunteer this information. Property tax rates are usually public knowledge and available on the city and county websites.

Be sure to add 2% to 3% to the mortgage price to get your estimated closing costs. To get an exact number, the lending institution is obligated to give you a "good faith estimate" that spells out how much you need to bring to the closing. When getting the cash advance, you might need to add these closing costs to the cash advance amount. If you don't use the entire amount of the cash advance, you can always return this to the credit card company.

Another thing you might need to add to the cash advance amount would be the cost of a home inspection. At this point in the game, there is no need for any surprises. A good home inspector can find all the items that need to be fixed. By all means, do not depend on the previous owner to tell you everything. A seller is obligated by law to disclose any items that need repair. Unfortunately, a seller can check the box labeled "no representation" and avoid telling you anything at all. This means the seller refuses to say anything at all. Does this mean there is something wrong? Not necessarily. Still, it does not hurt to ask why the seller checked the "no representation" box. Thus, a home inspection brings any and all material facts to the negotiation table. This allows you to make allowances for all the items that need repair and subtract that repair price from the asking price. If nothing else, the seller might volunteer to have the repairs done by a certain date. By all means, verify that the repairs were made and continue the negotiation.

Remember, we are only buying real estate because it is an asset that appreciates over time. That is a fancy way of saying that land increases in value as long as there is a demand for the land.

I Bought My House with Credit Cards

NEW HOMEOWNERS

When you get into your new home, do not buy any new furniture. In fact, leaving some rooms without furniture is perfectly fine. If you feel strange leaving some rooms without furniture, push a few boxes into that empty room. If people ask why the room has no furniture, tell them that you will get to the boxes in the near future. That room is now a "storage" room. Remember, you need all of your extra cash to pay off the cash advance.

Do you have empty cardboard boxes? Turn them into furniture. There was a famous architect back in the 70's who experimented with cardboard furniture. He discovered that he could stack up cardboard to mimic the shapes of chairs and sofas. This architect left the cardboard exposed, but this is not necessary. You can use a glue gun to adhere fabric to the surface of any exposed cardboard. In fact, there is whole cottage industry that makes "faux" furniture.

Why would anyone want to make "faux" furniture? Real estate agents say that homes with furniture usually sell faster than homes without furniture. Why? People can determine the length and width of a room much better when there is furniture in the room. As long as the furniture is similar in size to their own furniture, people can judge the size of a room based on the number of pieces of furniture in the photograph. Oftentimes, real estate agents take photographs of the rooms in the house before the previous owner moves out. Prospective buyers can determine the size of the rooms in the photograph based on the number and arrangement of furniture belonging to the previous owner. If the real estate agent cannot take photographs of the rooms before the seller moves out, the real estate agent may need to bring in "faux" furniture temporarily. Then, photographs are taken for advertising purposes. Why not turn your many cardboard boxes into "faux" furniture? From a security standpoint, you want criminals to think that someone actually lives in the house. Empty homes invite criminals and vagrants to break inside and vandalize the property. Worse yet, they could use your house as a base of operations to make and sell drugs.

The only items you may need to buy at the beginning are window treatments. Start with simple mini-blinds. Basic white is best. These are readily available at any hardware store. Some manufactures allow hardware stores to trim the mini-blinds to the correct length. Skip the plantation shutters and vertical blinds. Use heavy draperies only if you have large windows facing south. Excessive sun can be blinding. It can also make your HVAC unit work harder. If you have a single HVAC unit for more than one story, your HVAC unit will probably be working day and night. If you live in a cold climate and have large windows, get heavy draperies to keep the heat inside the home.

At least cover the windows if you can't have furniture in a room. In fact, close the door to the room and shut off the vents. There is no need to heat and cool any room that no one is using. For myself, I shut off all the vents that go into a room (or closet) that no one is using. You are just wasting money heating and cooling a room that no one is using.

Skip the house-warming party. People throw house-warming parties just to show off their new domicile. You can always throw a real party once you have furniture in every room. Besides, your neighbors, friends, and co-workers will just be snooping around your house during the house-warming party anyway. If they ask, politely say that you are undertaking necessary repairs. Promise them that everyone will get to see the new domicile once everything is finished.

Hold off on inviting family members or in-laws. If they drop by unexpectedly, hand them a paintbrush. Family members usually drop by unexpectedly because of their curiosity. Quench that curiosity by putting them to work. If they have a pick-up truck, tell them to drive you to the hardware store to pick up wallpaper, paint cans and gypsum board. I guarantee that your family members will think twice before dropping by. In fact, they may excuse themselves right away. Who really wants to work for free? Of course, let them help with the painting if they so desire. They will certainly turn around and tell the rest of the family to avoid your house.

If you have children, tell them that their friends are not invited to the new house. Your children's friends will be less discriminating when it comes to handing out derogatory comments. Don't host slumber parties or scout troop meetings. Your children may not like this, but your own children will be the ones who will be the target of scorn anyway. There is no reason to subject your children to this cruel treatment.

Next, hold off on the cable or satellite television. This is certainly a monthly drain. Usually, a new cable or satellite television subscription may require an upgrade to your television and their associated components. With the larger domicile, your old television set may look relatively small compared to the size of the room.

Audio-visual experts recommend that people should be seated a distance of six to eight times the height of the screen. Most televisions have a ratio of 4 units of width to 3 units of height. Widescreen televisions have a ratio of 16 units of width to 9 units of height. That means a regular 50" diagonal television will be 30" high. For a comfortable viewing distance, your sofa or couch needs to be anywhere from fifteen to twenty feet away. In short, you might not need to upgrade to that new 60" diagonal television after all.

When you upgrade your television, you most certainly need to upgrade your television stand or television cabinet. Hold off on the entertainment upgrades. Besides, you won't be able to watch much television anyway. You might need a temporary second job to pay off the credit card company. This means you will head to the bedroom to sleep after working two jobs. Your upgraded entertainment will probably go unused anyway.

Bring your brown bag to lunch and shop at the discount store. You won't be going out to eat

I Bought My House with Credit Cards

or enjoying any fine cuisine anyway. Skip the invitations to weddings and send them a gift card instead. You won't have time to attend anyway, because you might need that temporary second job. In fact, you might not be able to use your credit cards to travel anyway.

If you are married, watch how your spouse reacts to this difficult situation. Conversely, you can do the same to your boyfriend or girlfriend if you are not married yet. These will be tough times. Don't be surprised if your spouse or partner starts to complain. By all means, listen carefully and try to sympathize with their plight. Unlike previous generations, young people today have a special aversion to hardship. Their doting parents may have provided them with everything they so desired. Their parents may have shielded them from every difficulty in the interest of fairness.

Still, life is not about avoiding trouble. Hardship is a reality of life. Not everything will be sunshine and rainbows. If you watch your spouse or partner carefully, you will see exactly how they will handle adversity. If they can't handle this, there is little hope that they can handle more serious problems like death, cancer, long-term disability, or divorce. Pay attention to how they react. If you are not already in a serious relationship, it may be time to reconsider your future with this person. If it is your spouse, I do not recommend undertaking difficult tasks with this person in the future. You may be pleasantly surprised that this same spouse may make suggestions such as remodeling or putting in a new pool. When this happens, gently remind your spouse about how they complained incessantly after getting into the new house. This will usually squash further discussions. No doubt, your spouse may even downplay their behavior. Again, gently remind your spouse that you will not undertake any major life changes without further marriage counseling.

I Bought My House with Credit Cards

HOME EQUITY LINES OF CREDIT

After you are in the house for a few years, check on your credit card balances. If they are still high, look into getting a home equity line. A home equity line of credit may allow you to consolidate your debt into one neatly packaged monthly payment.

Be forewarned. Many lending institutions have discontinued offering home equity lines of credit.

How do you get a home equity line of credit? Usually, you will get an unsolicited offer in the mail from one of the local banks. By all means, call to see what they will need. Sometimes, they can pull up the information on your house. More often than not, the bank can pull your credit report. If they immediately turn you down because of the short length of time in your house, don't be upset. Politely ask how long you would need to be in the house to actually qualify. Perhaps the mortgage loan needs to be paid off to a certain extent. Usually, the bank will be glad to tell you. They might not be able to offer you any assistance for getting a home equity line of credit today, but there is always tomorrow. Take down the information and wait. If you have to continue the temporary second job to get to that magical percentage of mortgage paid off, do it.

After you get the home equity line of credit, pay off the credit card balances right away. Usually, the lending institution will give you a checkbook. Guard this checkbook with your life. If someone else (including a spouse or partner who loves to spend freely) gains possession of this checkbook, that person can usually spend the equity in your home in less than a day. Once those checks are cashed, you may not be able to get the money back. This home equity line of credit works like a credit card. Unfortunately, only credit card companies have the power to dispute fraudulent transactions. You don't have this protection when it comes to a home equity line. I recommend getting a fire-proof safe. Hide all of your important papers such as birth certificates, personal identification numbers, military discharge papers, divorce decrees, marriage licenses, and all the credit card checks from the credit card companies. Once you write the checks to the credit card companies, there is no other reason to use the checkbook from the home equity line. Lock the checkbook in the fire-proof safe and pay off the balance.

You will use the home equity line of credit as means to buy you some time. Usually, the home equity line of credit will have a lower interest rate because it is tied to the value of your house. As long as your house has some value, banks will allow you to borrow against the perceived value minus what is left on the mortgage.

Be warned that the bank giving the home equity line can cancel your available credit at any time. Yes, our home equity line of credit was canceled after real estate values plummeted in our neighborhood. Foreclosures popped up all over our side of town. Remember than home equity lines of credit are tied to home values. If home values drop like they did after the Great Recession of 2007-

2009, banks will be running away from any risks. If you were to foreclose on your house, the banks will not be able to recoup their money from your home equity line of credit.

FLIPPING

What is "flipping"? If you are not living in your newly acquired parcel of land, you can always turn around and sell the real estate. This is called "flipping". The idea is to buy a house that is in less-than-desirable condition at a lower cost. Then, the house is renovated to its previous glory and sold for a higher price.

No doubt, you have seen this on numerous television shows. Camera men follow the bold real estate investor as they find distressed properties. There is footage of the contractor valiantly repairing the property. They spruce up the yard. They repair the old siding. They replace the old rotten windows. They tear out the old kitchen appliances. The counter-tops are replaced with granite. Old plumbing fixtures are replaced with the latest sinks, toilets, and tubs from the hardware store. You might even see the particular hardware store prominently featuring their logo in the succeeding commercials and close-ups during the show. No doubt, the hardware store wants people to see their newest products and gladly donate their wares for promotional consideration.

Why are these television shows so popular? It is the "Cinderella effect". People want to see a dramatic transformation. Before the Great Recession of 2007-2009, people who had never picked up a hammer in their life started to think that "flipping" houses was as easy as watching television. Sadly, these people found themselves with overpriced properties in an economy where there were few buyers. Many eventually returned to their previous careers or declared bankruptcy.

What happened? Flipping only works in a booming economy. You are essentially buying real estate to sell at a higher price. For this to work, you need lots of buyers because that increases your chances of success. If you don't have a great deal of buyers, you will ultimately lower the price of your house to attract buyers. Simply put, it is the law of supply and demand. If there is a great supply of real estate available, the demand for real estate will go down. If the demand for real estate goes down, the price of real estate will eventually decline, too. If the price of real estate goes down, you might not recoup the money you paid to buy the property and fix it up. Many real estate investors lost millions in the Great Recession of 2007-2009. Don't be caught with properties that cannot be sold right away. Watch the financial news. Keep abreast of the prices of similar homes. Count the number of similar properties being sold in the area. If you don't know, ask a realtor or real estate broker. A simple phone call can clear up all of your questions.

Can you not find distressed properties in any economy? Yes. It is possible to find distressed properties in an economic boom, in a recession, or in a depression. The elderly and the aged may not have the financial means to renovate their own homes. As their health deteriorates, relatives may send the owners to a nursing home. The property may not be getting the regular maintenance or attention it deserves. Sometimes, distressed properties are not created by vandalism or vagrancy. Many people live in the same home for most of their adult lives. There was a time in America when people did not move from one city to another like we do today. There was a time when people worked in the same factory or business for decades. These people lived simple and humble lives. Thus, their outdated homes may need newer plumbing or additional toilet rooms. As long as the structure had no lingering defects, your renovation dollars went directly to the amenities that today's consumer would enjoy.

If you are planning on selling the homes right away (flipping), try to find the type of real estate that is the most popular. In New York City, this could be an apartment or condominium that is part of a co-op. These units make great rental units because they are situated in high density areas. There is a great demand for apartments here because of the many people who need to work nearby. Just make sure you are given the "covenants" or rules regarding the co-op. What do I need to know if I want to renovate? How is the unit heated and cooled? What utilities are provided by the co-op? Do I need to be interviewed before I can be allowed to buy into the co-op? Does the co-op have any restrictions? Do they allow pets and under what conditions?

If you live outside of a metropolitan area, try to find starter homes. Typically, starter homes are two to three-bedroom houses on small lots. They are usually less than 1,600 square feet. They may have a one-car garage or a carport. They have a modest kitchen. There may be two toilets, but there is usually only one bathtub.

Why get a starter home? A starter home is comparable in size to a two-bedroom or three-bedroom apartment. People who rent apartments will move into a starter home first because the cost difference is negligible. This is where former renters get introduced to the joys (and hassles) of home ownership.

If you want to rent out single-family homes, a starter home is the perfect size for people who normally rent apartments. Check the price of the apartment rentals in the area. If possible, price your single-family home to be comparable to the price of apartment rentals. If the monthly rent is higher, emphasize the amount of privacy the prospective tenant will get if they rent your starter home instead. Your prospective tenant will not have neighbors with blaring stereos on the other side of the wall. Your prospective tenant may be elderly with no desire for additional noise at all times of the night. Your prospective tenant may have young children and desire peace and quiet. If possible, offer to fence in the backyard in exchange for a larger security deposit. There are many ways to market starter homes because they are usually the next logical step for people who usually rent apartments.

Should I buy a starter home that has a homeowner's association? It all depends on what the homeowner's association demands. Always request the "covenants" to be given to you before closing. It should spell out all the requirements. If you don't like the requirements, don't buy the house. Most homeowner's associations are not very flexible. If nothing else, ask the homeowner's association about any renovations you want to make. It would be best to ask before you buy the starter home. You need to know ahead of time if you will be allowed to do what you want with the home.

I Bought My House with Credit Cards

Be forewarned. Do not buy homes where the tenants may have dabbled in the drug culture. There are new street drugs being created all the time. The ingredients for these street drugs may be hard to remove from building materials. At times, the toxins may be airborne and make its way into every nook and cranny in the home. Be sure to read up on their dangers. If you hear that your prospective property may have been involved in the manufacture of street drugs, make phone calls to the police. The real estate agent is obligated to reveal all "material" facts to the buyer. This means any information that may be admissible as evidence in a court of law. Be sure the real estate agent tells you if street drugs were manufactured in the home.

At times, the real estate agent may not be privy to that information. The seller may intentionally withhold relevant facts pertaining to the house. When in doubt, get a home inspection. Better yet, call up the local police department. Even if the seller does not talk, the police might know if there was illegal drug activity at that address. Keep asking questions until you get answers. Remember, you may be liable for damages if someone gets sick.

Former homes involved in drug activity may be intentionally destroyed by authorities. The parcel of land will be sold without the former structure. If this happens, you might be able to buy the parcel of land for very little money. You are then free to build whatever you want. True, you will need to abide by the local laws. If there is a homeowner's association in that neighborhood, check their rules and regulations. There may be limits to the maximum size of home. Setback requirements require the new structure to be built a certain distance away from the property lines. Ask the local planning and zoning if there are additional restrictions for that property.

On the other hand, having a few skills in the construction trades could be beneficial. If you want to "flip" houses, it helps to have friends or family members who are carpenters, plumbers, and electricians.

For example, a woman from New York City had a son who was a carpenter. She dreamed of owning her own apartment with her son in New York City. With only a minimum-wage job, she knew she would never have enough income to qualify for a mortgage on her own apartment.

In the paper, she discovered that several mobile homes were available just north of the city. Taking the train, she went to investigate. They found one mobile home that needed only superficial repairs. With her credit card, she took out a cash advance to pay for the down payment. As she worked extra hours to pay for the cash advance, her son spent his time making the necessary repairs. They moved into the mobile home and stopped paying rent for their apartment in New York City. Eventually, they sold the mobile home for a small profit. Instead of spending the profit, they used the money to make a down payment on a larger mobile home.

After living in the larger mobile home, they found a small house outside of the city. Her son did the repairs while she worked a second job to get extra money. Since they lived in each of the properties, they took the money they would usually pay in rent and paid down the mortgage. Also, they could wait patiently for a buyer that wanted to pay the right price. This was a price that would allow them to reap a profit. By living in the property, her son could do the repairs in his spare time. Since her son did the repairs, she was able to keep more of her money. The woman was careful not to spend any of the profits. Profits were used as a down payment for the next property they would buy.

With money in the bank, the loan officer was more willing to let them borrow larger sums of money despite her meager income. Eventually, she and her son moved up to her dream apartment. Years of working and saving had allowed her to achieve her dreams.

What were her keys to success?

First, they lived on the property. With this arrangement, they did not have both a mortgage payment *and* a rent payment. Since they were not paying rent, they only had the monthly mortgage payment and the cost of materials.

Second, they used "sweat equity". In other words, they did the repairs themselves to save money. Since they lived on the property, they were able to do the repairs as time and money allowed.

Should you always do the repairs yourself? Not necessarily, but repairs to gypsum board (often called sheetrock or wallboard) and trim can be done by anyone who can wield a hammer. Most able-bodied people can paint, too.

Electrical, HVAC, and plumbing repairs are a different story, though. Always ask to see a contractor's state license and demand proof of insurance. For first-time homebuyers, there is nothing wrong in going to the local big-box hardware store. Normally, these retail establishments can schedule licensed workmen to install electrical, HVAC, or plumbing. As long as you buy the components from their store, most big-box hardware stores let you use their credit card to pay the labor costs, too. Sure, the labor costs are not the lowest, but the big-box hardware store takes care of screening the workmen for you. Usually, the big-box hardware store guarantees the installation and normal operation of the unit, so you have somebody to call if things go wrong.

Personally, I have used the big-box hardware store card when I have replaced hot-water heaters and toilets during emergencies. If you don't want to use a big-box hardware store, always get three "bids" or price estimates from three separate contractors. It may take more time, but the savings may be larger, too. Don't be too surprised if the price estimates vary greatly.

Finally, the mother and son team saved their profits. Since they lived on the property, they could afford to wait for the right buyer. They could also wait for the right time to sell. When the economy was bad and no one was buying, they sat tight. They sold the property only when they knew they could make a tidy profit. They worked hard to keep money in the bank. Since she had a low-paying job, the loan officer would let her borrow larger sums of money based solely on the size of her bank account.

Of course, she had to borrow the down payment to get the first mobile home, but she took a calculated risk. No doubt, she was depending on her son's ability to make the necessary repairs. Not everybody is adept at the many facets of construction, but it could not hurt to start finding people who can help you. If you don't know the difference between a hammer and a hand saw, get to know a few carpenters. There are a good number of older men who have had to do their own repairs around the house. Your neighbor may know a thing or two about tools. He might even have woodworking tools. Don't ask to borrow his equipment. Just have a beer with him and ask him to show you a few pointers. You might be surprised at his willingness to be helpful.

The industry giant Henry Ford had friends that advised him about every aspect of his automobile before he even laid the foundation for his first factory. He cultivated friendships with people who had expertise long before he needed their expertise. To an extent, his friends were his mentors. Henry Ford's friends put him on the right path and helped put the pieces together for his dream.

Perhaps, it is time for you to get your "dream team" together. Let's face it. We only have so much time on this earth. Having people share their wisdom and knowledge with us could eventually save us years in the quest to fulfill our ambitions. Maybe you have wisdom and knowledge you can provide to these people in exchange. I remember having a friend who was a cabinet-maker. He built custom stereo speaker cabinets. There was nothing about woodworking that he did not know. I found myself in the wood shop with him when I had free time. He would ask me about drawing and drafting, and I would ask him about using the many tools that were in his shop. I still use that knowledge today and he was a good friend and mentor.

Do you have any mentors? If you want to be good at something, it is best to ask someone who has been successful. Do you want to "flip" houses? Do you want to buy and sell houses? It would never hurt to questions to someone who has been "flipping" houses. It may save you time and money. If nothing else, you will eventually know if this is right career path for you.

BEING A LANDLORD

If you don't want to buy and sell houses, maybe you would like to be a landlord. If you don't want to pay for the mortgage, why not let someone else pay the mortgage for you instead?

How do I know that the property is a good deal? Find the Gross Rent Multiplier. This gross rent multiplier is calculated by taking the market value of the property divided by the annual gross income. Obviously, market value is what people want to pay for the property. The annual gross income is the total amount of money from rent that the owner of the property should expect to receive. After you make the calculation, compare this Gross Rent Multiplier to a similar property nearby. If the number is close, the asking price of the property may be a fair price. If the Gross Rent Multiplier is lower than that of similar properties, the rental income is inflated. Do a quick check to see if the nearby rental rates are similar. If not, the current owner is inflating the expected incomes from rent. If the Gross Rent Multiplier is higher than that of similar properties, the asking price may not be a fair price.

True, the Gross Rent Multiplier is just another way to compare rental properties. A real estate broker should be able to give you the Gross Rent Multiplier on the property you want and the Gross Rent Multipliers from similar properties. If there is a huge difference between the numbers from all of the rental properties, watch out. In theory, the numbers should be similar, because rental properties in close proximity should be generating similar income and similar asking prices.

What if I don't want to be a "slumlord"? First of all, the author recommends having a well-kept rental property. You may need to sell the rental property at some point in the future, so it does not pay to have a rental property that is not presentable. Sure, you can save a few dollars by not keeping the lawn mowed or fixing the broken windows only at the last possible moment. On the other hand, a well-kept rental property might fool a burglar or vagrant into thinking someone actually lives in the house. If the grass is high enough to hide an automobile, people will automatically assume no one lives there. Be safe. Don't give unwelcome "guests" any reason to pick your rental house. If you can't be there, send some money to a neighbor so he can mow the lawn in your absence. Besides, the neighbor does not want the criminal element to pick your rental house either. If this is the case, the neighbor might even mow the lawn for a reduced price. I had a neighbor that would email me with complaints about my rental house. At first, the neighbor's emails were annoying. Later, I came to depend on that neighbor to know what was happening in my rental house. Remember, you (as the landlord) are going to be sued if someone gets hurt on your property. Remember, someone is bound to get hurt if there is criminal activity in your rental property.

As a landlord, you may be getting calls in the middle of the night. Once, I was sent to the house to fix a broken water heater. Upon inspection, I knew that someone had been tampering with the controls to the water heater. The control knobs had been torn off. Still, I had the plumber there the next day. I lost $300 and six hours of sleep, but everything was back to normal within 24 hours.

Please realize that there are many laws regarding the landlord and the tenant. Surprisingly enough, most laws protect the tenant. In fact, you can be sued by the tenant if you *do* act like a "slumlord". I realize that there are unscrupulous people in every occupation. If someone ever accuses you of being a "slumlord", they are probably ignorant of the many laws protecting the tenant. These are usually people who complain about their miserable lives to anyone who would bother to listen to them. What is my advice? Don't have these people as friends. They will only hold you back.

Since the majority of laws protect the tenant, my advice to you is to take a course in real estate. Most real estate classes are can be taken at the local community college and/or technical institute. The course should be less than $300. Sure, there will be general topics about what constitutes real estate versus personal property. These topics will eventually lead to the most important part of the course for you: property management.

What is property management? Simply put, property management is what you do as a landlord. A property manager can interview prospective tenants. Once the tenants are screened, the property manager will present the prospective tenant with a contract. They take security deposits and hold them in a trust account. Each month, a property manager collects rent from tenants. If maintenance is needed, the property manager will do the work himself or find qualified people to do so on his behalf. If there is any dispute, the property manager will represent the owner of the property by appearing in court. When the tenant leaves, the property manager will assess any damages done by the former tenant. If the damages are minimal, the property manager will deliver the remainder of the security deposit to the former tenant. If the damages are significant, the property manager may start legal proceedings to recoup some of the money.

Be forewarned. Many states will not allow you to engage in property management unless you are currently licensed by the state. This affords the state some measure of control over the activities of landlords. However, there is one common loophole. In most states, you can engage in property management if you truly own the parcel of land.

Why bother getting licensed to do property management? It is important for anyone engaging in the business of real estate to know what you can or cannot do. As I said before, most laws protect the tenant and not the landlord. You as the landlord will need to know your rights.

For example, let us take a closer look at the most important part of your job as a property manager: rent collection. Without rent collection, there is no reason for you to be a landlord. You want the tenant to pay for the mortgage and not you. True, you can charge whatever you want as a monthly rent payment. This monthly rent payment can be significantly higher than the mortgage payment. It all depends on what the market will support. If a tenant is willing to pay large sums of money each month, you should be willing to receive those sums of money as a property manager.

I Bought My House with Credit Cards

There are laws dealing with how you do your rent collection. In many states, you are not allowed to pick up the phone and harass your tenant. You are usually not allowed to call them at their place of work. There are laws outlining how soon you can start asking for rent.

Finally, there are laws dealing with rent that is late. This is when your knowledge of the law becomes crucial. When you study property management, all aspiring landlords should know how many days are needed before you can file for "summary ejectment". A summary ejectment is right of the owner of a property to start legal proceedings against a tenant who violates his contract with the property owner. (A summary ejectment can also be used to legally remove vagrants, squatters, and trespassers.) When a tenant fails to pay rent, the property owner must go to court in order to recover the rent payment. However, there are a set number of days between the time the rent is late and the first date the property owner can file for summary ejectment. This is often called the "grace period".

If this is not complicated enough, the property manager (or property owner) will have to post a notice in a conspicuous place. The notice will inform the tenant in no uncertain terms that the rent is late. Through experience, I have discovered how my tenants enter my rental house. Usually this is the side door next to the driveway. A simple letter-sized notice taped to the side door usually gets their attention. Of course, there is the alternative method provided by the United States Post Office. You can send a letter that requires a signature. The postman will ring the doorbell and have the tenant sign for the letter. With this method, you can have everything in writing. Since this will cost you some money, keep careful records of these costs. In the end, you may be able to deduct this from the security deposit.

From your real estate course, you will know how long the "grace period" will be. You can file for summary ejectment only after you made an attempt to give the tenant ample notice. During this grace period, there are laws that control the behavior of the property owner and/or the property manager. First, you are probably not allowed to make harassing phone calls to the tenant. You are absolutely forbidden to make phone calls to the tenant's place of work. Second, any harassing phone calls that are recorded by the tenant is admissible evidence in a court of law. This could work against you. In fact, it may prompt the judge to take action against you. If you have to make a phone call, be polite and be firm. In my experience, the tenant will try to avoid your phone call altogether. Actually, they might even hang up on you. When this happens, don't get upset. You can always bring this up when they call you demanding repairs to the property.

After you file for summary ejectment, let the courts take over. By all means, bring the lease and any other document the tenant may have signed. I am surprised how many landlords do not bring their signed leases to the courthouse. When you appear in court, be sure to shower and shave. Be in good spirits. Answer all of the judge's questions. Don't be surprised if there are many cases being seen that day. The judge will not have time for you to be fumbling through paperwork. Have the date that the rent was due. If you sent a letter to the tenant, have the receipt from the post office ready. If the tenant has a history of late payments, have the documentation ready.

By all means, do not get upset! Be mentally prepared to lose. Why? *Judges will usually give the benefit of the doubt to the tenant* . I know that does not sound fair, but you will soon discover this peculiar truth.

What should I expect? Do not be surprised if the judge does not demand the rent payment from the tenant. Sometimes, the tenant will not show up in court. This is usually in your favor. The judge will not look kindly on a tenant that does not show up in court. In some states, this could be construed as "contempt of court". Still, the judge will probably give the tenant an extra thirty to sixty days to make the rent payment. The judge will want to appear as "merciful" as possible.

What now? Wait. In my experience, the tenant will usually appear at your doorstep the night before the judge will allow you to reclaim your property. The tenant may even send someone else on their behalf. The rent money will be handed off to you. Of course, there will not be anything extra. The tenant will no doubt be late with their next rent payment. Still, the tenant will fulfill the judge's order to the letter and nothing more.

What if the tenant does not deliver the rent payment? You have to go back to court. You will get another court date. The judge will get the sheriff or constable to schedule a time for the eviction. By all means, *do not do this yourself!* Let the courts handle this. If you decide to evict your tenant without the court's help, you could be subject to criminal prosecution. Check the laws in your state. Be sure you know what you can do and what you cannot do. The last thing that you need is for your tenant to grab a ruthless lawyer that will sue you for everything that you own.

Can a tenant sue you for everything that you own? It depends on the laws of your state. This is why I recommend that you take a real estate class at your local community college. If nothing else, you will know exactly what a landlord (or property manager) can legally do. I recommend not giving a tenant any reason to hire a lawyer. Even if you do everything right, a tenant may have friends who will try to sue you just because they think you have money. Remember, most states hold the property owner responsible for whatever happens on their property. This gives unscrupulous lawyers an opportunity to sue you even though the tenant may be at fault. I recommend asking your insurance agent for umbrella liability insurance to cover unexpected lawsuits or general tenant negligence. If you do need to get umbrella liability insurance, I see no reason not to pass this cost along to the tenant.

What can I get the tenant to pay for? The tenant's responsibilities should be spelled out in the rental agreement. Most office supply stores will have blank rental agreements. If you are not comfortable writing additional items onto a lease, I recommend asking a lawyer.

What if I don't want to pay for a lawyer's help? First of all, I recommend making friends with a lawyer. Remember, there are different types of lawyers, so find a lawyer that deals with real estate. In my state, only a lawyer can oversee a real estate transaction. These lawyers are actually called real estate lawyers. Their title might be different in your state. Again, this is something you can easily learn in that real estate class at the community college. I recommend getting to know a lawyer *before* you even get into legal trouble. Ask friends or family members for referrals. Take the lawyer out to lunch and get their thoughts before you embark on acquiring real estate. You might be pleasantly surprised at the advice they can give you. Their advice might save you a lot of time, money, and heartache. Take lots of notes and keep their advice in the back of your head when you deal with tenants.

What can I add to a rental agreement? You can add anything you want to a rental agreement as long as it does not break any current laws. In fact, a rental agreement should spell out the address and location of your rental property. In my experience, I have seen landlords taking their rental agreements to court only to find that they put the wrong address on the rental agreement. Of course, the judge cannot enforce a rental agreement to the wrong address. In the end, the tenant was asked to vacate the property because they were now trespassing. On the other hand, the landlord could not collect any rent either. In fact, the landlord was asked to return the security deposit and the past rent payments. Eventually, the landlord and the tenant settled their differences out of court, but we can all learn a lesson here. Don't ever forget that the rental agreement (or lease) is a legal document. Be absolutely certain that the information is correct.

Make sure that you never sublet. Have a clause in your lease that the tenant can never allow someone else to rent the property from them. All successful rentals start with a tenant that pays on time. A tenant that does not pay on time will drain you of money faster than a teenager with your credit card.

Here are a few items to add to the lease agreement:

1. The lessee shall provide the lessor photo identification issued by a government entity. The lessee shall provide the lessor with credit information including but not limited to the lessee's Social Security number. The lessor shall report any delinquent rent payments to at least one of the credit reporting agencies after the lessee vacates the leased property.

2. The lessee shall not engage in the creation and/or distribution of controlled substances. Any such activity shall constitute a violation of the lease agreement. The lessor shall contact the authorities immediately if there is any evidence of illegal activities in or around the lease property.

3. The lessee shall abide by all local and federal laws regarding firearms and/or the discharge of any firearms. Firearms shall not be stored on the lease property unless express written permission is granted by the lessor. The lessor shall contact the authorities immediately if there is any evidence of illegal activities in or around the leased property.

4. The lessor shall change the air filters to the heating and cooling unit once each calendar month. Lessee shall provide access to the heating and cooling unit inside the leased property.

5. The lessee does not have the right to turn over the control of the property to a third party including family members of the lessee. The lessee shall have the stated property as their primary domicile. In the event that the lessee surrenders control of the stated property, the lessee will be in violation of this lease agreement. This includes but is not limited to the distribution of keys to a third party.

6. The lessee shall notify the lessor immediately regarding any flooding event due to nature, acts of God, or plumbing failure. This includes but is not limited to the overflow or malfunction of any sink, toilet, tub, washing machine, or dishwasher.

7. The lessor shall be notified in writing of any pets (including dogs, cats, reptiles, birds, etc.) residing temporarily or permanently on the premises. The lessor has the right to refuse aforementioned pet and a charge an additional fee not to exceed $100 each month. The lessee is responsible for any residual fecal matter, blood, vomit, secretions, and/or odor. The lessor has the right to charge the lessee with additional carpet cleaning, painting, or repair associated with aforementioned pet if the lessor has not charged an additional monthly fee.

8. The lessee has the right to make rent payments with revolving credit. The lessee has the right to guarantee the payment of rent with traveler's checks and/or similar check tied to revolving credit. The lessor does not have the right to use these traveler's checks until the rent is past due and the lessee is notified in writing. The lessee shall immediately notify the lessor in writing if the revolving credit is canceled to make alternative financial arrangements.

9. The lessor has less than six calendar months to complete any written request for repairs to the heating and cooling system. During this six month period, the lessee shall not initiate any legal action against the lessor. All repairs to the heating and cooling unit shall be made by approved technicians. The lessor will not reimburse the lessee for any repairs unless the repairs were initiated by the lessor. The lessee is not allowed to deduct the cost of repairs from any future rent payments.

How do I get a good tenant? Everything starts with the interview. There are websites for landlords that allow you to check a person's credit history. All you need is a social security number.

Can I really ask a prospective tenant for a social security number? Yes. As a landlord, you are essentially running a business. *This is a fact I cannot stress enough.* Businesses ask for social security numbers all the time, and you should, too. What if my prospective tenant balks at my request for a social security number? Politely thank them for their time and show them the door. Once, I had a tenant who did not want to reveal their social security number. As it turned out, this husband and wife team moved from rental house to rental house between two states. They never paid more than a month or two of rent. They waited until the day before the sheriff was scheduled to arrive so they could move. They had a sordid history of moving from place to place. In fact, the husband and wife had criminal records that included check fraud and weapons violations.

Don't be afraid to run a criminal background check on your prospective tenants. Don't be fooled by appearances. Be sure to call their most recent landlord. Be sure to call all of their character references. Don't be surprised if these character references are actually family members who help perpetuate the criminal activities of the prospective tenants.

Be forewarned that most landlords do not report bad tenants to the credit reporting agencies. As a landlord, you are running a business. There is no reason why you cannot report your bad tenant to at least one of the credit reporting agencies. Bad tenants seem to know this and move from place to place in an attempt to defraud at least one more unsuspecting landlord.

What if the prospective tenant does not want to tell me who the identity of their most recent landlord? Politely thank them for their time and show them the door. If the prospective tenant asks why this information is important, inform the prospective tenant that you are running a business. You are not running a charity. You can give them a list of addresses to homeless shelters in your city ready for them.

Don't be too surprised if your prospective tenant does not give you a recent address. If you suspect that a prospective tenant is not living at the address, ask to see their driver's license. In fact, *insist on getting a copy of their driver's license.*

What if they do not want to show me their driver's license? Once again, politely thank them for their time and show them the door. Sure, liberal politicians balk at having people show their photo identification at the polls. In the name of fairness, they want everyone to vote, with or without photo identification. Still, everyone *does* have photo identification. All fifty states have some way that allows people to get photo identification with little or no cost. Usually, this photo identification is available from the same government agency that provides driver's licenses.

Don't ever forget that you are running a business. Business people ask for photo identification all the time. Would you sell alcohol to a young person without asking for photo identification? No, because you can be liable for whatever the young person does with that alcohol. In the same way, would you allow a complete stranger to occupy your rental property? You will ultimately be responsible for any damages they do to your rental property. If you don't get the correct information on your prospective tenant, you cannot file legal action against them. There's nothing worse than going to court only to discover that your tenant gave you bogus information. Trust me.

I Bought My House with Credit Cards

You will be the laughingstock of the courtroom.

What if the prospective tenant says there is a law against showing a landlord photo identification? This is where your real estate class comes handy. Confidently, you can ask the prospective tenant to return with that information (or misinformation). Don't be surprised if that prospective tenant never returns. Even if the prospective tenant returns, you can see exactly why the prospective tenant has this erroneous belief. Don't be too surprised if this information comes from a dubious source.

As a landlord, you will be confronted with all manner of misinformation. It is your job to know the law that applies to renting out real estate. You don't need to know the law word for word, but it helps to have friends you can call if you have questions, too. Don't be too surprised if your bad tenant knows more about landlord-tenant laws than you do.

As a matter of fact, criminals usually pass along this information to family members. It is no big mystery that older inmates pass along their "trade secrets" to younger inmates in prison. I had a tenant who sublet our rental property to a drug dealer. I should have known by the tack marks around the windows. No doubt, the windows were covered each time drugs were sold. To avoid the authorities, drug dealers may lure cash-strapped tenants. As we said before, don't allow anyone other than the tenant to live in your rental property. *No subletting at all.* Make sure that is spelled out in the lease agreement. In fact, read the lease agreement in its entirety to the prospective tenant. If the prospective tenant has any problems with any of the items, the prospective tenant needs to voice their concerns before anything is signed.

Remember, it is always harder to remove a tenant than it is to acquire a tenant. Once you turn over your keys, your financial well-being is in the hands of the tenant. I cannot stress enough that you need to choose your tenants carefully. If you can't find qualified tenants, lower the monthly rent. It is far better to get a tenant that pays on-time with a lower payment than the alternative. The name of the landlord game is to have someone else pay for the mortgage. What is the use of a higher monthly rent if you never receive the cash?

At some point in time, being a landlord may become easier. As we discussed earlier, the internet is creating new ways of doing things all the time. Eventually, there will be a way to automatically take the rent from a tenant. There won't be any more phone calls to the tenant about late rent.

Should a landlord or property manager accept credit cards? Personally, I have looked into the possibility of taking credit cards, but my tenants have not been receptive to the idea. Let's face it. All you need is their credit card number. Each month, you can immediately make a credit card transaction to get the rent money. My local bank sent me a flyer advertising their credit card processing service. Usually, there is a steep set-up fee. Still, the swipe fee seemed reasonable. Nowadays, there are smart-phone applications that let you process credit cards. All you need is their smart-phone attachment.

If you do take credit cards, it should be part of the lease agreement, so the tenant has no way of stopping the credit card purchases. In the lease agreement, you would stop these automatic rent payments after they have vacated the premises. No doubt, your tenant will make haste to leave the property and turn over the keys. Sure, your tenant can cancel the credit card. Still, you can have a clause in the lease saying that canceling the credit card will violate the lease. Of course, this means the tenant no longer has any incentive to vacate the premises in a timely manner.

Instead, a landlord should ask for "alternative" forms of identification. When someone writes a check at a retail establishment, that person is asked for a credit card number. The card number is written on the actual check.

Why do merchants ask for a credit card number when writing a check? Some credit reporting agencies have services that allow a merchant to verify addresses. The merchant enters the credit card number and a billing address will appear. Why is this useful? Merchants can easily track down people who write bad checks.

Remember, you are not doing this because you operate a charity. Remember, criminals do not want to provide credit card numbers, because credit reporting agencies keep close tabs on their true billing address. If nothing else, the credit reporting agencies can tell you if these credit card numbers are even valid numbers. If you have any doubts, ask to see the actual card. Be sure to make photocopies of both sides.

If your prospective tenant won't show their credit cards, ask for the credit card checks that the credit card sends with their statement. There is a good chance your prospective tenant will not provide you with the credit card checks either. No doubt, their credit card information will be on the credit card check. Be sure to get them to write a month's worth of rent on the amount. Don't forget their signature, too. If possible, ask for two credit card checks. This will tie you over until the sheriff arrives to give them the eviction notice.

Law enforcement may not have direct access to this information, but you (as a legitimate business owner) will be able to track down people who write bad checks. Consecutively, you turn over their billing address to law enforcement when you file for summary ejectment. Imagine the surprise on your former tenant's face when law enforcement serves them a subpoena at their billing address.

What if the prospective tenant does not want to provide me with credit card numbers? This might be a danger sign. In truth, a prospective tenant that does not have credit may not be a good credit risk at all. Sure, your prospective tenant may say that they do not have any credit cards. Kindly inform your prospective tenant that you will be checking their credit report as a part of the interview process. At this point, your prospective tenant may turn and head for the door. Let them leave. Criminals do not want anyone to check their arrest record, much less their credit report. Remember, their credit reports should have current billing addresses. They can also have past addresses as well as any alias.

On the other hand, your prospective tenant may admit that they don't have good credit. They may have cut up their credit cards in an attempt to pay off debt. If you are presented with this situation, take the time to listen to their story. You will get clues to their creditworthiness. In fact, you might decide to show them the door. Why? You are running a business and not a charity. The last thing you need is to listen to a new sob story each time the rent is due.

Ask your prospective tenant how they intend to pay the rent. Do they have extra income? Do they have an inheritance or a trust fund? Is there any proof of any of this? If you don't get all of your questions answered, you certainly won't get any of your rent money. If you get a sob story, you will certainly get more each time you ask for the rent.

Why go through all of this? In reality, you need to weed out all of the charlatans. Bad tenants come in all shapes and sizes. From personal experience, my worst tenant was well-dressed and very personable. He had everyone fooled. We had no idea about his prior weapons violations and check fraud. We would never have thought that he was a criminal.

Yes, there are people out there that work to polish their image. This is most evident in politicians. Movie stars and reality show celebrities spend entire lifetimes cultivating an image that people want to see. Don't be fooled by outward appearances. Ask for their driver's license. Ask for their social security number. Tell them that you will pull their credit report. Tell them you will check references and criminal records. If your prospective tenant balks at any of these requests, demand to know why. Remember, you are operating a business. You are entering into a contract with a prospective tenant. If they don't take your requests seriously, you can bet that the prospective tenant will not treat your requests for rent with any seriousness.

Should I accept Section 8 tenants? Yes. Section 8 is a government-run, government-sponsored program that provides rent subsidies to lower-income people. Unfortunately, many municipalities are finding it harder and harder to provide these subsidies. Like many government-run programs, there is a great deal of abuse. Many unscrupulous people take advantage of this program despite the fact that they have the means to pay the rent themselves. Oftentimes, those participating in this program have jobs that pay in cash. Since these people are paid in cash, the government cannot verify their true income and allow these people to continue receiving the rent subsidies.

When you interview prospective tenants, you may be approached by a prospective tenant that has a Section 8 voucher. There should be a dollar amount on their voucher. Remember, the government will not provide you with a cent more than that dollar amount. That dollar amount is not negotiable. The dollar amount is based on the number of family members. The dollar amount is based on the local rents and is adjusted yearly. If you accept this person as a prospective tenant, the government will contact you and send you the appropriate paperwork.

I Bought My House with Credit Cards

Be forewarned. Your property will be inspected by local authorities. The government will only grant the rent subsidy after making sure the rental property is up to their standards. In fact, your rental property may not qualify for Section 8. The government will send a building inspector to the house, so make sure everything is in working order. Make sure there are no cracks in the windows. Make sure the sheetrock is smooth with no cracks or evidence of mold. They will check all the plumbing and the electrical. The building inspector may ask you to upgrade the electrical or HVAC system. If you have an older house, you might think twice about accepting Section 8 tenants.

With Section 8 tenants, the government will deposit the rent subsidy directly into your real estate trust account. You will get a paper copy of the electronic deposit in the mail. Since the Section 8 tenant is interviewed every year, the government may lower the amount they deposit. As the landlord, you may be informed in writing about the change, but it is up to your Section 8 tenant to ask for a larger subsidy. Some municipalities limit the amount of time a Section 8 tenant receives a subsidy. This is not good if your Section 8 tenant has no other means of income. Before you accept a Section 8 tenant, check if they have additional means of income that you can verify. Remember, child support and alimony payments are never guaranteed. Since the dollar amount of the Section 8 voucher changes, insist only on Section 8 tenants who have a steady job.

Finally, never have a family member or friend as a tenant. If they ask, tell them that you are running a legitimate business. That being said, explain to them that you cannot imagine asking them for rent money. You want to continue to be friends with them. You don't want to be the cause of any family strife. Do your best to dissuade them from even thinking about renting your property. Why? Most people have a hard time asking friends and family for money. Worse still, most people do this specifically so they *can* get free rent. I realize there are arrangements between family members that do work. Usually, these involve parent-child relationships where the parent will not allow any tomfoolery. Remember, you are running a legitimate business and you need someone who pays on time.

Do I need to have a business license? If you own the rental property, you are free to rent out the property to anyone without needing a business license. If you own the house, you can rent out a room without having to get a business license. In fact, some property owners rent out their empty rooms for cash. The rooms may not be rented all the time. In fact, the cash amounts are so low that the property owners use the money for maintenance costs.

Do you have a spare bedroom? If you live near a college, you can rent that spare bedroom for a small fee. Of course, you may have to provide a separate entrance. Make sure that your tenant has separate toilet and bathing facilities. I remember renting a room in Connecticut. Someone had converted an old Victorian home into four apartments. There were communal facilities on both floors so you only had to share one bathroom with another tenant. If you are a plumber, you can easily find a way to turn a single-family home into a duplex by adding plumbing fixtures for two tenants. You can even borrow the renovation money by using a hardware store credit card. If you have children that have moved away, why not put that extra square footage to better use? That can be extra income you will need in retirement. In this day and age, Social Security only provides a meager existence. If you get the rent payments in cash, you can choose not to declare this additional income.

Do I need a license to collect rent money for other people? In most states, you have to be a licensed real estate professional to do property management if the property does not belong to you. Let's face it. Municipalities need some way to regulate rent collection. Since most landlord-tenant laws protect the tenant, municipalities want to make sure tenants are not unduly harassed. Tenants don't need burly men showing up at doorsteps demanding rent money. Thus, municipalities want to license all individuals who collect rent for other people.

I realize that many books and movies portray landlords as ruthless men who hire unscrupulous thugs to shake down innocent tenants for the rent money. True, today's landlord-tenant laws originated from the disputes involving New York tenement buildings. Tenement buildings housed most of the poor immigrants that came to the big city. Since the poor immigrants were considered second-class citizens, the tenement building owners used lawless means to obtain their rent money. Unfortunately, their methods of rent collection became so blatantly notorious that laws were enacted to curb the abuses.

I highly recommend taking the real estate class at your local community college. Be sure to ask the instructor the best ways to collect rent. Can you call the tenant at their place of work? Can you record phone calls between you and your tenant? Can you charge late fees? Can you apply the late fees to the security deposit? How much of a security deposit can you demand? When can you enter the property? Can you enter the property to a make a repair without the tenant's knowledge?

From personal experience, I found a wonderful way to see what was going on inside the rental property. Every month, I went to the rental house to change the filters on the HVAC unit. Sure, it was an inconvenience, but it allowed me access to the rental house. I made sure this was in the lease. Still, I would have someone call over to the tenant. I would state a time and date I would arrive at the property. I did not need my tenant pulling a gun at me. I also forbade pets in the rental house. I did not want the tenant getting a belligerent dog (that would use my leg as chew toy).

At the rental house, I would knock on the door. I would say in a loud voice that I was there to do the maintenance. If I didn't get an answer, I would unlock the door. If no one was there, I would repeat once more that I was there to do the maintenance. Usually, there was somebody there. Sometimes, they were in their pajamas. Sometimes, the kids would show us to the HVAC unit.

True to my word, I changed the filter. At the same time, my wife would ask the tenant for the rent money. Notice, I had my wife look around while I changed the filters. If your tenant is a single female and you are a male, be sure to let the wife look around. If you are not married, have your girlfriend look around. If you don't have a girlfriend, you can always ask a female friend or coworker to do the snooping for you. You don't want your female tenant to get a restraining order against you. Be sure to reimburse your female friend or coworker for their time.

As a landlord, you should always check to see if your tenant is doing anything illegal. You would be surprised at what a tenant would try to do. For example, your tenant could unfasten all of the light fixtures and sell them at the flea market. They can rip up the floors and sell them to another homeowner. Personally, I had a tenant kick a toilet with such force that the toilet was no longer fastened to the floor. Sadly, they tried to repair the toilet with tape. When the sewer smell became too much, the tenant finally gave us a call.

When your tenant moves out, don't be too surprised that the refrigerator is no longer usable. At this point, the power company may have already turned off the electricity. For this reason, I recommend talking to the utility companies before this happens. Make sure the utilities are put back in your name once the tenant vacates. As it turned out, there was no way to remove the stench of rotting food in the refrigerator. Eventually, we threw out the old refrigerator.

On top of that, we discovered that sink disposal unit had quit working a long time ago. On the sink itself, one of the handles had been replaced with an adjustable wrench. In the bathroom, our tenant had removed the large mirror from the wall. The tenant even took the bathroom shower rod and the medicine cabinet.

Back in the kitchen, the tenant had oftentimes complained about the dishwasher. Eventually, the tenant decided to replace the dishwasher on their own. I had promised to reimburse them for the cost of the new dishwasher. In the end, the dishwasher was the cleanest thing in the house. I suspect the tenant found a used dishwasher. Sadly, the tenant did not know how to install the old dishwasher correctly and the dishwasher remained completely unused.

One day, I arrived at the house to see kitchen cabinets stacked at the end of the driveway. Fortunately, the kitchen cabinets belonged to the elderly woman next door. After placing their mother in a nursing home, the elderly woman's children ripped out everything from the inside of the house.

This is why I highly recommend that you have a way to check the inside of the rental property. Make sure it is part of the lease agreement. If the prospective tenant balks at this part of the lease agreement, thank them for their time and show them the door. The last thing you need is to get a call from local law enforcement on the subject of illegal activities in your rental property.

No doubt, the tenant will remove all evidence of mischief during your visit, but the extra work might be too much for the tenant. It may even cause the tenant to change their mind about doing any criminal activities on your property. Remember, you are ultimately responsible for what happens on your property. If the tenant is dragged into court, the tenant will ultimately feign ignorance, so be sure to protect yourself.

That being said, I recommend holding off on any repairs until the rent is paid in full. Even the most elusive tenant will call you when something breaks. When the rent is late, I will only make repairs when there is flooding in the house. For example, my tenant complained about wet floors. I drove to the house as soon as I left work. As it turned out, the washing machine leaked each time it was running. I was not sure where the tenant bought the defective washing machine. Still, I had to stop the flooding. As we all know, flooding causes wood to rot. Wallboard soaks up water like a sponge. Eventually, you will see water stains at the bottom of walls. Luckily, there was not much water on the floor and the tenant promptly wiped it up with a beach towel.

Pay attention to the tenant's phone calls. If they say "flooding", be sure to investigate right away. Most homeowner's policies don't cover flooding. Flooding is usually covered with a separate policy.

On the other hand, repairs dealing with heating and cooling should be treated differently. Why did I choose to change the air filter for the HVAC unit each month? A tenant that does not pay their rent on time cannot be trusted to change the air filter on time, either. If you can't trust someone with rent, you should not trust them with maintenance. HVAC units are expensive. Don't forget to include the annual cost of HVAC maintenance when you calculate the monthly rent payment. These are costs you should pass along to your tenant.

Remember, your rental property HVAC unit always breaks down during the hottest time of the year and the coldest time of the year. This is because the HVAC unit is being used more often during these times in the year.

First, make sure the condensate line is clear. What is a condensate line? An HVAC unit has a cooling mechanism that lowers the temperature of hot outside air. All air has a certain percentage of moisture. During the process, the cooling components on an HVAC unit will make contact with moisture-laden air. As a result, droplets will form. These droplets are collected in a pan underneath an HVAC unit. Sometimes, a float valve is located in the pan. When there is an overwhelming amount of water in the pan, the float valve will open. This allows the droplets to escape down a "condensate" line. Make sure you pour bleach down this condensate line. Microscopic organisms love growing in dark, moist areas. Over time, these organisms can choke off condensate lines. A little bleach can keep these organisms in check.

Where is the condensate line? Usually, the condensate line starts at the pan underneath where the moist air turns into droplets. Usually the pan is at the bottom of the HVAC unit. The condensate line could be made of copper or PVC pipe. A condensate line made of PVC pipe should have a place where you can dump bleach into the condensate line. Usually, this part of the condensate line is capped. Just unscrew the cap and pour in the bleach. The HVAC manual may even tell you how often you should flush the condensate line. When in doubt, pour a cup or two of bleach (like the ones you buy for your laundry) in the springtime.

The condensate line should eventually lead to the outdoors. Make sure there are no obstructions. Trim away any weeds or high grass nearby. Plants have been known to block the end of condensate lines. The condensate line provides fast-growing weeds with a constant source of water during a drought.

Second, look for the electrical disconnect to the HVAC unit. Usually, the electrical disconnect is outdoors near the condenser. The condenser is the outside component of the HVAC unit. It has a fan inside that runs when the HVAC unit is in operation.

Why should you know the location of the electrical disconnect? You need to turn off the unit completely after you call for maintenance. Your tenant will continue to run the unit even after the vents stop sending cool air inside. Don't be too surprised if your tenant tries to restart the fan motor with a stick. Be sure to inform your tenant that you are turning off the unit. If there is no electrical disconnect, you may have to trust that your tenant will do the right thing and leave the HVAC unit alone. At this point, remind your tenant that they are not allowed to touch the HVAC unit. Remind them in writing that the tenant will be charged for any additional damage to the HVAC unit. Usually, this is enough to keep them away.

In some cases, your tenant may think they can fix the HVAC unit themselves. Don't be too surprised if your tenant gets electrocuted. If this happens, start looking for a new tenant. No doubt, their family lawyer will be looking to sue you. This is when you present the lawyer with the written request to leave the HVAC unit alone. Usually, this is enough to keep the lawyer away.

What if they have not paid the rent, but they want me to fix the HVAC unit right away? I had a tenant who insisted that we fix the HVAC unit. The tenant had not paid the rent. It was in the middle of hottest summer in years. No doubt, our tenant was calling constantly with complaints about the heat. Politely, I asked about the late rent. Our tenant told me in no uncertain terms that she could sue me for not having a functioning HVAC unit. Politely, I explained to her *(what I learned in real estate class)* the dwelling was still habitable. As a landlord, I would be responsible for making sure my rental units are habitable. This included providing adequate indoor plumbing. As far I knew, there was running water in the house and all the toilets and tubs were operational. Politely, I explained to her that air-conditioning is a luxury item. Most of the houses built before World War II had no air-conditioning. Logically, air-conditioning is not a requirement to make the house habitable. In fact, you should have a clause in the lease agreement stating that the HVAC repairs will be made only when all rent payments are current.

As it turned out, the tenant moved out. No doubt, they literally could not take the heat. To no one's surprise, I never received my rent money. If that was not bad enough, my tenant asked for her security deposit back. In reply, I gave her a rundown of all the damages to the house. The damages alone exceeded the amount of the security deposit. Needless to say, there was dead silence on the other end of the line. To this day, I am still waiting to be paid back for all the damages to the house.

I Bought My House with Credit Cards

What have we learned here? Know the law. Unless the house is flooding or the plumbing is not working, don't pay for any repair until you get your rent money. You are only responsible for having a habitable dwelling. Air-conditioning, satellite television, internet access, draperies, carpeting, laundry machines, dishwashers, ceiling fans, sheds, and electricity are all luxury items. In fact, utilities should be paid by the tenant. Don't ever volunteer to pay for utilities. You will lose money faster than a bad gambler in Las Vegas. The only time you should even think about paying for utilities is when you are renting out a room.

When you *do* collect rent, be sure the rent money goes into a separate bank account. In some states, all rent deposits need to go into a real estate trust account. When you take the real estate course, ask the instructor where rent payments need to be deposited. These real estate trust accounts may or may not cost extra, but be sure to follow the law. You do not want the judge to rule in favor of your tenant just because you did not use a real estate trust account. There may even be penalties if you do not follow the rules regarding rent deposits

From an accounting standpoint, you should never mix your money with your tenant's money. This concept is called "commingling". In some states, a real estate professional can lose their license if they start mixing funds from a tenant and their own funds. Imagine trying to point out to a judge which deposits belonged to the tenant and which deposits belonged to you. It would be very embarrassing having the entire courtroom peer into your personal spending habits. With some bank statements, it may be impossible to know for certain who made what deposit. I once had a tenant that paid her rent with whatever change was lying around in her house. I suspect she was digging through her couch when it came time to pay the rent.

Save yourself the time and hassle. Keep yourself out of jail. If need be, pay the extra cost of the real estate trust account. Keep your personal deposits and your tenant's rent deposits separate. Pay the mortgage payments using checks assigned to the real estate trust account. This will show the judge that you have nothing to hide. Besides, you are operating a legitimate business.

Do I need to have C Corporation or a Limited Liability Corporation? I recommend asking your tax professional that question. Personally, I had a C Corporation. However, I could not accept any rent deposits or disburse the monthly mortgage payment unless the C Corporation owned the rental property. The IRS has special rules about rental properties. These rules also include depreciation for tax purposes. I do not recommend using H&R Block™, Jackson Hewitt™, or any of the consumer tax preparation services advertised on television. Find an accountant that does tax preparation. It will cost you double what the consumer tax preparation services charge, but you will save money in the long run. Don't bother doing the taxes with any of the software packages you can get at your local office supply store. Let a professional accountant do the work and let them represent you if you are questioned by the IRS. Don't fight the IRS alone!

Use standardized forms when you contact the tenant. These forms are readily available at the office supply store. If not, there are internet sites that cater exclusively to landlords. Save yourself time. If there is a cost for the forms, be sure to include that with the proposed rent payment.

If you do get a tenant that does not pay, be sure to make that fact known to the credit reporting agencies. Give them a call and see how you can file a formal report. This may cost you more money, but you can be certain that your former tenant will have a harder time renting a house anywhere else. In fact, your former tenant will have a hard time renting from an apartment complex. If that is not bad enough, automobile rental companies may start asking your former tenant more questions. Even though you may never see it, your former tenant will be feeling the effects of his or her actions long after you've sold your rental house to someone else.

A former tenant of mine refused to show up in court. Since my former tenant was ordered to pay the late rent, this late payment turned into a judgment against the former tenant. There is now an outstanding warrant for his arrest. I am sure my former tenant still lives nearby. If the police ever pull him over, my former tenant will probably spend the night in jail. No doubt, the outstanding warrant will show up on his police report. I may never see my money, but I don't have any qualms about sending my former tenant to jail. My former tenant had his opportunity to talk to the judge, but he refused to show up.

I Bought My House with Credit Cards

WHAT IF I DON'T QUALIFY FOR A LOAN?

What if the bank or credit union says I don't qualify for any loans? It happens all the time. Was I hurt when I was turned down for a loan? Sure, I was hurt by the rejection. I am only human. Still, the loan officer's sole job is to make sure you can pay back the loan.

Before you leave the bank or credit union, be sure to ask the loan officer just why he or she turned you down. Be polite. Don't be antagonistic. Have a genuine interest in what they have to say. The truth will hurt, but this is not about your current feelings. You don't ever want to be in this situation again. Take a deep breath. Put your pride to the side. Take notes. This information will help you in the future.

At this point in the process, it would help to know why you did not qualify. Whatever you do, smile! This is invaluable information. Evidently, the answer might not be what you want to hear, but you need to know this information. Being turned down for a loan is not the end of the world. Just know that you will be asking for loans in the future. Your job after a rejection is to knowing *why* you were rejected. Remember, it is impossible to win if you don't know why you lost.

Resist the urge to walk out on the loan officer. Insist on knowing what you need to do to improve your chances of getting the loan next time.

Naturally, you will think that the loan officer is too critical. Remember, the loan officer's job is to make sure the person asking for the loan has the ability to pay the loan back. It is their job to assess your creditworthiness. Typically, the loan officer is not attacking your good name. Sad to say, most loan officers just see a credit score. They are not obligated to know any more besides your creditworthiness.

Are you trying to ask for that million dollar mansion with your minimum-wage job? Take a step back and start small. You always have time to upgrade. You need to show the loan officer that you can pay all of your financial obligations on time. Why not start with a small starter home? Wait until your career starts to take off. Save a stash of cash and find a larger home later.

Do you have too much debt? If your total credit card debt is larger than the value of your car, there is a good possibility you are in over your head. As hilarious as this sounds, I am speaking from personal experience. After my divorce, my credit card balances exceeded the value of my car. Sadly, my net worth was less than zero. In fact, I lived in that car. Everything I owned was in that car. If you find yourself in this situation, go get help. Luckily, a local charity had a credit counseling department. These wonderful people negotiated with my creditors on my behalf. It took me a full six years to pay off all the outstanding balances. If I can do it, I am sure you can do it, too.

Everyone goes through good times and bad times. Unfortunately, bad times have a way of impacting our ability to pay our financial obligations. For me, my divorce devastated my good credit. You may have had an unscrupulous ex-spouse, too. Your spouse may have left the marriage in shambles. Since you and your spouse share the financial responsibility, the credit card companies will no doubt go after both of you. If your spouse decides to skip town, you will be left to pay the debts. I know that this is not fair, but this happens all the time.

If you are newly divorced, don't be so hard on yourself. Get yourself to a reputable consumer credit counseling service. Make sure this is a non-profit consumer credit counseling service, because there are a lot of charlatans that prey on desperate people.

A good credit counseling service will negotiate with the credit card companies on your behalf. They will stop the collection calls and get you on a payment plan. It might not be any fun, but the results are fantastic. In fact, my credit score was much higher   *after* the non-profit credit counseling service helped me. Why? The credit card companies saw that I was able to fulfill all of my financial obligations. I demonstrated with my actions that I was trustworthy. To the credit card companies, trustworthy means creditworthy.

If you are newly divorced, give yourself a few years to get your finances together. Be sure you *are no longer financially connected to your ex-spouse.*   Close those joint accounts. You and your ex-spouse may be paying on a house or car together. If these financial obligations were not handled by the divorce lawyer, get rid of these financial obligations right away. Sell the house. Trade in the car. Do whatever you need to do to end these financial obligations.

What if I have no way to pay for my credit card bills? I recommend reading Kevin Trudeau's Debt Cures™ "They" Don't Want You to Know About. I wish I had his book fifteen years ago. There are some surprising facts and sophisticated techniques for unburdening yourself from the shackles of credit card debt.

Did you know that most people have an average of $8000 in credit card debt? Did you know that most people have an average of eight credit cards? Did you know there is a statute of limitations for revolving credit? Yes, there is a point in time when a credit card company will have to stop trying to collect from a consumer. After reaching the statute of limitations, you can simply inform the credit card company that they can no longer collect on the debt. Even if you have *not* reached the statute of limitations, you can always keep silent and wait patiently for the time to expire.

Are you really sure you owe that much? Are you really sure you are talking to the right credit card companies? Debt collectors are notorious for masquerading as lawyers, government officials and the credit card companies themselves. Are they really are who they say they are? Have the caller send you the information in writing. Don't be too trusting. By all means, *don't admit to anything*. Have the caller prove their case. Whatever you do, don't send them any money until you know for certain. Even then, you might not have any money to send them.

I agree with Kevin Trudeau. Having a statute of limitations for revolving credit is probably the best thing that the state governments have done to curb the abuses of the consumer lending industry. With billions in profits, the consumer lending industry is depending on an uninformed consumer not knowing their rights.

For example, I live in the great state of North Carolina. At one point in time, I had $30000 in credit card debt from my divorce. After contacting a lawyer, I discovered that the credit card companies have no more than three years in which to file suit against me in civil court to collect on the $30000. In theory, I could wait three years until the time expires. The credit card companies have that time to file suit against me in civil court.

I had already cut up my credit cards and my ex-wife's credit cards. I was no longer doing business with these credit card companies. The clock starts ticking for the credit card companies. Of course, I cannot buy a house, finance an automobile, take out a loan, or get a credit card in the meantime. Remember, your old credit card companies will be monitoring you credit report. As soon as you try to buy anything that requires credit, your new address and contact information will show up on your credit report. When your old credit card companies see this, they might track you down and take you to court. No doubt, the new credit card companies will show that you defaulted on the old debt. Even though I could have easily avoided paying for the $30000, it was better for the sake of my credit report to pay the $30000 off slowly in the long run.

If you have questions, pay a lawyer to see what rights are afforded to you by your state. Your rights are there to protect you. Whereas the credit company will just write off your debt as a loss, your outstanding debt will haunt your credit report for years to come. If the debt is a mistake, contact the credit reporting agency immediately. You are entitled to one free credit report each year. Check the list of creditors. If you don't recognize a company on the creditor's list, give the company a call. Most credit reports have mistakes. For me, my ex-wife still tries to get credit cards in my name even though we have been divorced for almost two decades. The last thing you want to do is to pay for someone else's debt.

When you read Kevin Trudeau's <u>Debt Cures™ "They" Don't Want You to Know About</u>, you will discover that the statute of limitations for revolving credit is three years in the states of Alabama, Arizona, Arkansas, Delaware, Washington D.C., Kansas, Louisiana, Maryland, Mississippi, New Hampshire, North Carolina, Oklahoma, South Carolina, Virginia, and Washington. You are quite fortunate if you live in these states. Next, the statute of limitations for revolving credit is four years in the states of California, Florida, Georgia, Idaho, Nebraska, Nevada, New Mexico, Ohio, Pennsylvania, Texas, and Utah. You may have to hide in your parent's basement one year longer.

Next, the statute of limitations for revolving credit is five years in the states of Illinois, Iowa, Kentucky, Missouri, Montana, and West Virginia. Five years is a long time to be hiding from the credit card companies. You might even have to trade-in your present automobile (for a lower-mileage version).

Next, the statute of limitations for revolving credit is six years in the states of Alaska, Colorado, Connecticut, Hawaii, Indiana, Maine, Massachusetts, Michigan, Minnesota, New Jersey,

I Bought My House with Credit Cards

New York, Oregon, South Dakota, Tennessee, Vermont, and Wisconsin. A great deal can happen in six years. You might even be starting a new family. More than likely, your current spouse will probably be divorcing you. With no new home and no new automobiles in six years, many spouses might just throw in the towel.

Finally, the statute of limitations for revolving credit is ten years in the state of Rhode Island. If you live in Rhode Island, I recommend paying off the credit card debt instead. It may take you less time to pay off the credit cards than it would be to wait ten years for the debt to reach the statute of limitations.

If you are just starting out, don't be so hard on yourself. Someone who does not have a credit history is always a gamble. There are people who receive their first credit card and immediately go on a shopping spree. These people don't realize that they are spending money they eventually have to pay off. Sometimes, they think their parents will pay off the credit card for them. Unfortunately, many parents do. These young people have no concept of the value of money. In most school systems, there is little or no financial education. No one tells the young person about using credit cards.

If you are just starting out, make sure you have steady employment first. Then, go to any of the large department stores. Fill out an application and send it off. Use it a few times and pay off the entire balance each month. I guarantee you that you will have your choice of any of the non-department store credit cards. The offers will hit your mailbox by the handful. Pick one or two applications. Send the applications back to the credit card companies. I recommend no more than one of each of the major credit card issuers. Use a few and pay off the balances each month. Don't be tempted to use these over and over. This is where most people get in trouble.

After that, go to a car dealership. Ask to see the smallest car they have. Remember, this is about building your credit. This is not about filling your garage with the most expensive sports cars money can buy. I don't recommend doing this without steady employment. In fact, this might backfire if you don't have steady employment. The car dealer will ultimately turn you down and report this to the credit reporting agencies. You don't want this to happen.

Why are we getting the smallest car on the lot? You still have to pay for insurance, taxes, and gas. If you are just starting out, a car payment can destroy your meager income. If can ride a motorcycle, you might be better off buying a motorcycle instead. On the other hand, motorcycle insurance in some states may be cost-prohibitive. Make a few phone calls to your insurance agent first. If your budget is really tight, you may have to settle for a moped. The idea is to have a car, motorcycle, or moped payment. Make sure that the financing company reports to a credit reporting agency. Some financing companies don't send reports to any of the credit reporting agency, so don't forget to ask. Don't be surprised if the salesman doesn't know.

After that, send off the car payment (or motorcycle payment) off each month. Pay off the balances on your credit cards. If necessary, work extra hours or get a second job. After two years, you should be ready to buy some real estate. On the other hand, your personal situation may have changed dramatically in two years. You might not be buying real estate for just yourself. You may be buying real estate for a wife (or husband) and child, too.

Always remember that loan officers are people, too. Borrowing money is serious business. Experienced loan officers may have already seen someone who had a similar credit and job history. That loan officer may have seen others like you default on a similar loan.

Personally, I have talked with loan officers who have asked me to reconsider my desire to get a loan. In fact, the loan officer thought it was a bad idea. As it turned out, the loan officer was right and I learned a valuable lesson that day.

I Bought My House with Credit Cards

FORECLOSURES

If you don't pay back a loan, you can be sure that this mistake will be on your credit report for at least seven years. When people can't pay back the loan, people usually let the house go into foreclosure. Unfortunately, foreclosure is not as easy as mailing the bank your keys. In fact, banks do not want the keys to your house. Banks don't want to be landlords. Before jumping into real estate, you need to know what happens when things go wrong. The Great Recession of 2007-2009 was a surprise to many people, and this can happen again. Before we go any further, let us look carefully at what we want to avoid: foreclosure.

What is foreclosure? According to Bruce Harwood's <u>Real Estate Principles</u>, foreclosure is "the procedure by which a person's property can be taken and sold to satisfy an unpaid debt". In short, the borrower fails to continue paying the home loan (mortgage). The bank goes to court to seize control of the real estate. After the court approves the seizure, the bank sends someone to the house to change the locks and place a "do not enter" sign on the door. A real estate agent is assigned to sell the house. If the house is not sold right away, the bank may auction off the house for pennies on the dollar.

For the most part, banks make money only when you pay your mortgage on time. In fact, banks lose money when they get a foreclosure. Banks make money on the interest on the loan. They don't make money when the house is put up for auction. They usually lose money when the property is sold at auction. Usually, the bank will write off the defaulted loan as a loss. Unfortunately, the borrower has to live with this foreclosure on their credit report for a very long time. This results in higher insurance premiums and higher interest rates for any loans the borrow gets in the future. This could add up to a lot of money over time.

By law, the government is the first one to get their money from the sale of any foreclosure (or any real estate for that matter). In fact, the property tax is always the first thing paid on any real estate transaction. The next creditor to receive money is the institution that carries the first mortgage.

Yes, there can be more than one loan on a house. The next creditor to receive money is the bank or lending institution that made the second mortgage. Before 1984, the requirements for the second mortgage were the same as the first mortgage. After 1984, the government limited the money that be drawn on a second mortgage to be less than half of the first mortgage. Government rules for second mortgages were not in place until 1981.

Finally, the lending institution (that provided the home equity line of credit) is next in line to receive money from the real estate sale. This means the lending institution providing the home equity line of credit will have the highest risk of not being paid back.

Should I buy a foreclosed home? No, because time will not be on your side. Foreclosed homes need approval from the many people at the bank and/or any investors that have a stake in the home's ownership. There may be legal issues with the previous owner. The previous owner's rights may or may not have been terminated. The previous owner could still appear in court to challenge the judgment. This process may take months or years. In my own neighborhood, many houses sat empty for years due to the foreclosure process. If you really to want to pick up some bargains, I recommend getting to know the loan officers and/or personnel involved with foreclosures at your favorite bank. Most banks and lending institutions don't want the general public to know about their foreclosures, so don't be surprised if they don't reveal anything to you. On the other hand, they might just have you buy some of their foreclosed homes if you have the financial resources to get their homes off their books. Don't be surprised if they want the full price of the home.

Before you buy, have the home inspected. If the home has been sitting vacant for years, you may have lots of repairs ahead of you. There was a foreclosed home in our neighborhood where the previous owners left their dogs in the house. I suspect the dogs were there to keep the bank from repossessing the home. The stench from their fecal residue made prospective buyers vomit on the front lawn. Probably, the buyer ended up replacing all the carpets in the home.

In the end, the bank or lending institution may not want to deduct the cost of these repairs in the purchase price. Remember, these banks and lending institutions are in the business of making a profit. In the end, the foreclosed home may not be a bargain after all.

I Bought My House with Credit Cards

BANKRUPTCY

Please do not get the mistaken notion that all credit card debts are discharged in bankruptcy. You probably have friends that have gone through bankruptcy. Since credit card debt is unsecured debt (debt that is not backed by any collateral), the credit card companies are the last to get paid. Bankruptcy court will usually ascertain what can be sold from our belongings. Usually there is nothing left for the credit card companies to receive, so the credit card debt is discharged. However, do not assume that the credit card debt is *automatically* discharged.

In fact, large cash advances made within a certain period of time may not be readily discharged in a bankruptcy. The credit card company may sue you for fraud. No one wants the public to know your lavish spending habits, but the credit card company will display this in court. If this happens, you won't receive much sympathy from the judge. In fact, you will be treated like a criminal. Usually bankruptcy court is there to help the consumer find a way to pay back his or her financial obligations. If the credit card company starts to think they will not get reimbursed, there is no reason to think that the credit card company will quietly discharge your financial obligations. Instead, they will try to prove that you had no intention of repaying anyone. Before the Great Recession of 2007-2009, people in bankruptcy court were given a fresh start. After the Great Recession of 2007-2009, people in bankruptcy court may serve jail time.

To make things worse, credit card companies may even sue you before bankruptcy court. If they think you are in financial trouble, the credit companies may take legal action right away.

From personal experience, you do not want to be on the wrong side of the credit card companies. They will call your work every day until they get their money. After my divorce, the credit card companies kept calling my work so often that I almost lost my job. If you don't pay the credit card company right away, they will send your debt to a collection agency. The credit card company employees were usually adamant about when they will receive a payment. In contrast, the collection agencies were just belligerent. Don't be too surprised if their language is much worse. Collection agencies are not above using profanity.

Even if you are not behind on any of your financial obligations, it is important to keep track of all your revolving credit card debt. After my divorce, I had credit companies calling me that I did not recognize. If you don't recognize the credit card company, politely ask them   *who* signed the application form. To my surprise, my ex-wife had taken out credit cards at all of the major retailers in town. Of course, I was listed as one of the card holders. The credit card company assumed that I was paying the bills because I was the head of the household. I told these credit card companies that I never signed anything. By law, there was no signed consumer contract. Politely, I asked these credit card companies to show me an application with my signature. To this day, I was never shown a copy of any contract I ever signed with these credit card companies. Eventually, these phone calls stopped.

I Bought My House with Credit Cards

GETTING RICH THE RIGHT WAY

The purpose of this book is not to get rich quick. Buying and selling real estate is not a get-rich-quick activity. In fact, buying and selling real estate is slow. Let's compare buying and selling real estate to other activities such as buying and selling stocks. Companies have computers that buy and sell stock at the blink of an eye. These companies have sophisticated algorithms that determine the exact moment to purchase securities and trade them for maximum profit. This is not the case with the buying and selling of land. Men have fought and died for land. The ownership of land is considered sacred. The importance of land will always be part of the human experience. Thus, real estate will never be a fast way to riches.

In the same way, the purpose of this book is not to have the largest house one can afford, but that is certainly possible. No, the purpose of this book is to at least have a place for you to retire. Having a home to call your own means you do not have to throw your money away on monthly rent. Let's face it. At some point in time, you have to retire. After retirement, you will not be taking home a monthly paycheck. Without a monthly paycheck, how are you going to pay for rent? It would be better if you had a place to call your own. You need your own piece of real estate. It could be a small apartment in New York or a cabin in the woods of Alaska. Either way, you will not be homeless. It is a shame that some people end up homeless after a lifetime of work. That is the biggest reason for this book.

At this writing, the minimum wage is $7.25 an hour in my home state of North Carolina. At age 85, a person earning minimum wage can amass over a million dollars in earnings. Evidently, this assumes he or she works forty hours a week starting at age 18 and gets paid vacations. He or she has no bills and pays no rent or taxes. Of course, we all know that situation does not exist. We all have to pay for food, clothing, shelter, and taxes. These are unavoidable expenses. In large metropolitan areas, the costs are even higher. It is no surprise that people in large metropolitan areas have more than one job just to make ends meet. That being said, a minimum wage job will not allow most people to achieve the goal of having their own domicile. That is the reason one has to use some form of leverage to achieve the goal of owning a plot of land. That is the second biggest reason for this book.

Next, I do not want people to get caught in the "consumer" trap. I realize consumption of goods and services is a large chunk of the United States economy. Still, there is no need for you to get ensnared by the endless parade of gadgets, automobiles, and entertainment. Sure, you need to eat, but there is no need to go overboard just to impress the neighbors with your choice in restaurants. There are better ways to show that you are successful. Even if you are successful, do you really want the neighbors to know? If the neighbors know you have valuable stuff, the criminals know that, too.

A long time ago, a wise man told me that you need to be the one selling the tickets and not buying the tickets if you ever hope to be rich. Unfortunately, the consumer lending industry does not allow credit card holders to purchase real estate or stocks. Why is this? I suspect the consumer lending industry wants the average person to spend money on items that have no lasting importance. Have you seen their commercials? They want the average person to purchase airline tickets, hotel rooms, and expensive vacations. Why do you think their reward programs are geared towards purchasing airline tickets and the latest gadgets? For once, I would like to see credit card reward programs that pay for closing costs and dividend-paying stocks. At some point in time, the American consumer will throw up their hands in defeat. They will balk at all the high fees and cut up their cards. Unfortunately, it will probably be in the wake of another Great Depression. By that time, it will be too late for everyone.

The last reason for writing this book is because I want people to have a better future. Yes, I went through the nasty divorce. I lost everything. I received the nasty phone calls from the collection agencies. I felt so alone.

However, it does not need to end that way. Debt is not all bad. Consumer lending can be used for *good* purposes. The credit card companies want you to buy now and pay forever more, but you can purchase assets that *increase* in value. You can find a good place for your family. You can find that perfect retirement place. You just need to change the way you do things.